Lin Sheffrin was born in 1951 in Stratford, East London. After a successful twenty-year career teaching Modern Languages in a secondary school, she completed a Diploma in Counselling and has spent the last eleven years working with children who have emotional and behavioural difficulties. She has had several articles published in the *Times Educational Supplement* and has contributed to *Counselling in Different Settings* (published by Palgrave Macmillan, 2004).

Lin is a proud mother and grandmother who lives on the Isle of Wight with her second husband Chris. When she's not writing she enjoys swimming, cycling, playing guitar and dabbling in painting.

In the summer of 2007, Lin was diagnosed with colon cancer. Her story continues in her blog – please log in to *http://coloncancerdiary.blogspot.com/*

Published in paperback by Silverwood Books 2008
www.silverwoodbooks.co.uk

Some names have been changed in this account
to protect the client-counsellor relationship.

ISBN 978-1-906236-05-2

British Library Cataloguing in Publication Data
A CIP catalogue record for this book is available from the British Library

Set in 10pt Goudy by SilverWood Books
Printed on acid-free paper by LSUK

Fifty/50

A Memoir

by

LIN SHEFFRIN

SilverWood

This book would not have been possible without the support of my subscribers:

Christopher Nye
Rachel & Jonathan Gray
Levana Gray
Ziva Gray
Batsheva Gray
Daniel Sheffrin
Gerald & Teresa Chevin
Judy Sadler
Paul Sheffrin
Neil Proudfoot
Linda Coffey
Geraldine & Cliff Jones
Sabine & Meinhard Jaster
Gillie & Dave Rhodes
Sharon & Herb Gray
Janet Julian
Lynda Jennings
Margaret & Bryan Nolan
Amy Gold
Julie Swaney

This memoir is dedicated to

My children, Rachel & Daniel

My grandchildren

My devoted husband Chris

and to the loving memory of

My parents and grandparents

Contents

Prologue

Dearest Grandchildren,

We are generations apart but bonded by love. We have led quite different lives yet will share no doubt the same emotions: joy, sadness, fear, anger, apprehension, confusion.

In these memoirs I have attempted to capture a kernel of what it has felt like at times in my life to be me, in the hope that the essence of what I once was will leave a footprint in your lives. If any of it helps any of you along the way, then all the better. There is a poem 'Success' usually attributed to Ralph Waldo Emerson, which has a haunting line in it:

To know even one life has breathed easier
because you have lived.

My grandparents and my parents have all passed over, and I so wish they had left me some diaries or letters which might have given me a taste of their lives; the bit I never knew. I want to make sure therefore that I leave you with something very special. Some sketches from my life, some funny, some poignant, some frightening, but all true and without exaggeration, that I promise you. Be aware that in writing them I held to the thought of you one day wanting to read them at age sixteen, fifty-five or even eighty.

My life has not always been easy. There have been smooth and happy times, and dark rocky times when it felt as though I was stuck in a tunnel of despair. It is the love and support from my closest family and our ability to laugh unreservedly at ourselves and with each other that has helped me through. I have every confidence that you will all experience that love, support and laughter for yourselves. I don't believe life was designed to be easy, but we are given the inner strength to meet our challenges.

Please enjoy my memoirs, and may they give you as much

pleasure in reading them as they have given me in writing them.

Pass them on to your own children; they are a social history of the Fifties and Sixties in particular.

Take care as you go through this life. I will always be with you.

Blessings,

Grandma England

Beginnings

The room where I sit is quietly comfortable. Sunlight floods in from the large patio door. The Dorset stone tiles lend an air of calm to the environment. The cupboards tables and doors are all different woods; oak, walnut and teak. Each of the eight paned windows has teak frames. The Yucca plant reaches upward to the ceiling. The settee and armchairs blend with the cool grey and autumnal brown shades from the flooring. Notebooks and paper are scattered on the oak coffee table. CD's sit neatly in the wooden rack adjacent to the patio door. The walls are picked out in magnolia. Outside there is a cacophony of bird sound. The neighbour has an aviary with exotic breeds. The large crows and gulls that circle the distant rooftops occasionally drown their sweet song. Harry joins in with his short sharp barks, and our neighbour Jeanette tries to reason with him and her cat William.

"Come on, William. Come down from there! Harry, leave William alone. Oooh, you naughty boys."

From my armchair I can see the Queen Anne throw that I crocheted when I was pregnant with your Uncle Daniel. It is in thick Mercer cotton, slightly rough yet silky to touch. The larger floral displays are of deep rich ochre, interspersed with four petal flowers in white. The whole cloth has a fluted white border.

I look over at the cloth and reminisce. It is time for me to begin.

It seems I owe my existence to a domestic tiff. After my brother Gerald was born in 1948, Dad was adamant. No more children! Gerald had been premature and was not expected to survive. His very early childhood was plagued with illness and there were many times when he was close to death. My Mum, however, had other thoughts. She did not want an only child; she craved a daughter.

In early Fifties post-war Britain money was tight and a lot of home improvements were DIY. Mum and Dad were decorating the bedroom, which was largely a success until they decided to paper the inside of the cupboard to match the rest of the room. Problem was, Dad forgot to size the walls in preparation. He had mixed a bucket of paste in readiness. Mum stood by helping. All appeared well until he was applying the second sheet of paper. He had to stretch across and catch the first sheet, which was gracefully unpeeling itself from the top left hand corner. Undaunted, Dad re-pasted the initial sheet and carried on. At first his reflexes were quick and he was coping reasonably well with Mum's help. Gradually however, as more and more sheets went up, an increasing number fell down. By this time Mum was helpless with giggles and really no use at all. Dad was getting hot under the collar because Mum was laughing so much she couldn't hold the paper any more. In his haste Dad managed to step off the ladder and plunge one foot into the paste bucket, causing him to slip. I understand that as he collapsed onto the floor the paste bucket toppled over and he ended up flailing around in a sea of slime unable to stand up. Dad reached out to catch hold of Mum's arm to steady himself, but still laughing uncontrollably, she fell on top of him.

The rest I will leave to your imagination. So it was that nine months on, the 15th of January 1951, at 5.15am, I entered this world, loved and wanted by at least one parent.

Diary – bad news

Oh, Grandma. Where are you now when I need you the most?

The doctors draw a curtain round the bed. Mr E's voice is solemn. "We removed a tumour from your colon, which has spread into your liver. We took out fifteen lymph nodes, six of which were cancerous."

It is hard to absorb the news. Harder is the relinquishing of control of my life. I have had major surgery on my bowel, and face an operation on my liver as well as chemotherapy.

I don't know how this will affect me. I am scared. Strangely it is not the fear of death. I am terrified of pain and suffering.

A month ago I was apparently fit and happy, working full time, swimming in the sea, cycling, and living life to the full. My world has been transformed. I have lost more than a stone in weight. I am confused, very sick, and totally powerless. It's the worst nightmare for a control freak like me. It hurts to do just about everything. I walk slowly like an old person. I watch slushy movies on TV. I worry that my brain is going to mush. After thirty years in education I will not be returning to work. I don't know if I have the strength to get through this. How long do I have? What are my chances? There is so much fear and uncertainty.

Being trapped in Hospital takes some getting used to. At my lowest point I beg the nurse who is administering the anti sickness medication.

"Can't you give me something to put me out of my misery?"

I don't want to survive.

"Oh no. We can't do that. Too much paperwork!"

I have to smile.

I came into hospital with my dignity, but swiftly lost it. When you have to get mobile, but need to carry your own catheter like a handbag across the ward and everyone can see your pee, it is hard to feel properly human; more like a zoo exhibit. The puncture wounds from all the blood tests and failed venflons have left my arms and hands painful, black and blue. Hard enough not to be able to use stomach muscles, but when both hands and arms are swollen the indignity and powerlessness are just too much.

I am only 56 years-old. I look in the mirror at the scar. The twenty-two staples are gone now, but the vertical line from just below my breastbone to my abdomen looks crooked and ugly. I resemble one of Frankenstein's failed experiments. My stomach is still swollen with fluid. What have they done to me? Intellect reassures me that they saved my life, but I feel violated. Sometimes I cry like a baby. I have three grandchildren. Will they ever get to know me and love me? I would want so much to be a good Grandma to them all, but they live thousands of miles away in Canada. Will I ever be well enough to visit them?

I think about my own maternal Grandmother, Rose. She was disabled and a virtual prisoner in her flat above the shop. The steps were too hard for her to negotiate and her only trips out were about twice a year to our house for birthdays and Christmas. The rest of the time her surroundings did not change. I find myself wondering how she coped. I have been prisoner for a month, she was prisoner most of her life. Yet she was the wisest person I have ever met and I loved her dearly. She couldn't take me anywhere and didn't ever 'play' with me. None of that mattered. I adored her. She had answers to all my problems. She was never moody or snappy. I would love to draw strength from her right now. I can remember her at the shop so vividly.

190 The Grove, Stratford

It was always exciting to visit the shop. It was Grandpa's business. There was a large glass frontage, with bold lettering: ALTERS, Alterations Repairs, Cleaning, Pressing. In the window display were price lists, pictures of tiny-waisted ladies in suave grey pencil skirts and single- breasted jackets next to gents wearing smart pin stripes. Mum would carefully wrap garments in brown paper and pull string from the infinite ball under the counter.

Once, Ethel the cleaner took Gerald to Stratford Broadway.

Halfway there someone tapped her on the shoulder: "Excuse me. Your little boy...!"

She turned round to find that unbeknown to her, my angelic-looking brother had grabbed the end of the string and was pulling it behind him. Half a mile of string draped along the pavement and linked him to the shop. Poor Ethel had to haul it in on her return, shamefacedly winding it back as she walked, avoiding the strange looks, wry smiles and pointing fingers.

I walk in through the large glass door. There's a fitting room on the right. Behind the counter is a doorway leading the busy work- room. Alf gives me a cheery, "Good morning." He is incredibly tall and thin, his hair of purest white, his eyes pale blue and watery. There is a soggy brown stained roll-up permanently attached to his narrow lower lip, which moves up and down as he speaks, and which never seems to leave his mouth as he deftly sews cloth to lining. He probably should

Grandpa outside shop (1960)

have retired years ago. Co-worker Annie is tucked away in the corner, glasses perched on the end of her neatly chiselled nose, head tilted in concentration towards the dress she is repairing. It's called "invisible mending" and Annie is an expert. Uncle Colin wets a large grey piece of cloth and wrings it out stretching it over a pair of trousers. He lifts one of the flat irons from the fire. As the heavy iron comes down onto the wet cloth there is a loud hiss and a swathe of vapour rises to the ceiling, the smell reminiscent of steam railways. Annie takes her garment to one of the sewing machines and rhythmically works the treadle, easing the material through. In the centre of the room is a huge table with swatches of material of different shades, plain and patterned. There are boxes of buttons, needles stuck into fat stuffed cushions like mini aliens, pins holding unfinished sleeves and waistcoats tenuously together, and rails round the outside for the dresses and suits awaiting alterations. In a cubby hole in the corner is the all-important black telephone with its chrome dial.

"Maryland 4395, Alters the Grove. Can I help you?" Mum's voice sounds posh, but clearly it is one of the locals on the other end, because she soon resorts to the East End vernacular she can summon at will to help her customers feel at home.

"All right dearie. I'll 'av it ready by Friday."

I fly up the steep winding stairs to the kitchen; a magical room because Grandma is always there.

Grandma was crippled many years ago, and can only walk really short distances across the room with a stick. She can't manage the staircase down to the shop easily so very rarely goes out. She doesn't sit in an armchair, because it is too difficult for her to get up, so she never has a proper lap. Mum tells me Grandma was run over by a car; not until I am an adult do I find out the real reason she is disabled.

The best thing about my Grandma is her pleasure in seeing me. As I dance in through the door, flush with excitement her face lights up with the warmest smile. Grandma is usually cooking something delicious. There's that familiar wisp of grey hair clinging damply to her forehead. She is wearing a pinny, which is grimy with toil, its pattern faded with old stains from splashed gravy. Pots are bubbling on the stove and the appetising smells of roasting meat and potatoes fill the room. The lack of mobility has caused Grandma to become quite heavy. I often wonder why she gets hungry, because to me she always looks full.

There's a green gas stove on high legs on the far wall, next to a butler sink and in the middle of the wall is the black leaded range where the kettle of water sings quietly. The small fridge stands alone near the door, with a metal strip in the bottom corner that says KELVINATOR. I practise endlessly trying to say it backwards, because ROTANIVLEK sounds exotically foreign.

The focal point of the room is the table against the opposite wall with generous flaps that open up and a large starched white cloth that bears witness to Grandma's delicious apple pies. Gram lets me help making pies and cakes. She peels the cooking apples and slices them into fat chunks, allowing me always to eat a few sprinkled with sugar. Grandma always leaves a generous scraping of cake mix in the bowl for me, where Mum insists on cleaning out the last dregs. Oh, how Grandma spoils us. She sends Gerald and me to the baker's for a loaf. I remember the first time we were entrusted with this errand

"Now Gerald, I'll give you sixpence. I want you to walk round to Ellis's and ask for a large crusty Farmhouse. Look after your sister and don't forget to cross at the crossing!"

We queued in the baker's, our mouths watering from the tantalising smell seeping from the hot ovens. When it was our turn we took the loaf wrapped in thin white paper. It was so fresh that as we held it the warm loaf caved in under the pressure of our fingers, and of course we just had to break off a small bit of crust to try. It tasted so superb that we each tugged a little of the white doughy centre and devoured it greedily. Grandma wouldn't notice, we reasoned, as the outer crust was still intact. Unable to resist, every few steps we extracted a little more from the fragrant yeasty centre. Arriving back at the shop, we went up stairs and handed over what initially looked like a loaf, until Grandma held it. She quickly realised that the loaf was mostly hollow. Instead of being angry, Grandma just laughed.

"My, oh my!" she exclaimed, shaking her head with feigned surprise. "I do believe the mice have got into this one. Best buy me another."

Opposite the stairs is the enormous lounge, which overlooks the busy street below. There is so much heavy traffic on the Grove that the whole shop shudders as if there's been a mini earthquake each time a bus or a lorry goes by. The floor in the lounge has a wall-to-wall multi coloured floral carpet. The settees and armchairs seem huge. They have some sort of really thin vinyl covering which is starting to disintegrate and provides me with hours of entertainment as I pick it off. Gram never minds. If it does no harm and makes me happy then she is happy. I wonder if she realises why her candlewick bedspread is becoming increasingly threadbare. I love to tug the individual threads through the holes and stockpile them in colourful little heaps. Grandma hasn't a house-proud bone in her body!

There are two steps up to the toilet in the hall and another few leading to the top floor. The bathroom is vast, and sparsely furnished. The floor is covered with blue chequered lino. There's a free standing bath along one wall, a large rusty tank in the far corner and a cupboard. It makes a great echo chamber. Next door is the room that frightens yet fascinates me. Gerald and I call it the 'old room'. The first time Gerald coaxed me in there – "Come on Linda… Wanna see the old room?" – it wasn't exactly a choice.

I pulled back, hesitant, but he firmly took my hand, and hauled me inside. There was a dull yellow bulb in the ceiling, the only light source, and no windows. A horrible musty smell of dust and old newspapers was all around, and the place seemed crammed with trunks, and boxes.

What absolutely sent the goose bumps shooting round my body were the tailors' dummies, like headless corpses, some with tape measures hanging from them and some with pins where Uncle Colin had used them for fittings. My eyes were beginning to adjust to the gloom when Gerald gave me a shove, turned out the light and shut the door. It was so pitch black that nothing not even an outline was visible. I was terrified.

I hate the room thereafter, but venture in for the occasional dare.

Grandma and Grandpa's bedroom, which I love, is at the end of the dark corridor. It smells of Yardley perfume and I'm allowed to sort through Grandma's treasures, boxes of dress jewellery, and a beautifully carved hairbrush and mirror on the walnut dressing table.

Grandpa is a great character. He teaches me my first French words by reading aloud the label on the HP sauce bottle: "*Cette sauce superieur...*" When his tea is too hot, to Gram's annoyance he pours it into the saucer and drinks it from there to cool it down. He fought in the trenches in the First World War. Grandpa got sent home as his chest was affected by mustard gas. The injury saved his life. The rest of his regiment perished at Ypres. Gramps never talks about it. When we ask him: "What was it like in the war Grandpa?" a distant look comes into his eyes and he immediately changes the subject.

Every week Grandpa gives Gerald and me a small bag of three-penny bits as pocket money. Then as a treat Grandpa says: "Go next door, and bring me a block of ice cream and a bottle of R Whites."

We don't hesitate, because Grandpa makes the most mouth watering sodas you could imagine. In each tall glass he places a generous dollop of thick yellow Cornish ice cream and pours on the cream soda so that it sizzles and foams. We then suck the creamy sweet bubbly mouthfuls through a straw. Divine.

Weekends are always peaceful. Grandma sits in her upright chair and carefully segments her 'afternoon orange', deftly removing the pith and allowing the zing of citrus to fill the room. She always has time to listen as I chatter about my problems and usually has a wonderful piece of advice that helps melt them away. Once a week our peace is disturbed by Grandma's visitor. I know her as Aunty Ena. She rockets into the room and words tumble endlessly and rapidly from her mouth. The effect is like a whirlwind. I rarely understand much of what is said, but Grandma tells me that Ena is like a daughter to her. I probe with my questions, but am told only that Grandma and Grandpa adopted Ena when she was ten years-old and brought her up as their own when Ena's Mummy died.

What I loved best about Grandpa was his sense of humour. He wrote me funny letters, which were in an interesting code. The youth of today think texting is a new phenomenon. Gramps had it to a 'T'.

2 Y's UR 2 Y's UB, I C UR 2 Y's for me.

He would spend ages taking me on 'walks round the carpet', which were such fun. We pretended that the floral pattern was a beautiful garden and he described the beauty of the flowers to me in infinite detail. It captured my imagination.

"Can you smell that lily? It's a wonderful perfume! Look at those beautiful roses over there. You can pick one if you like."

Once a week he took me on a real walk. This would be round the 'back doubles' as we called it, past Windmill lane and over to the Coach and Horses pub. Grandma knew he liked the odd pint, but didn't really approve of his drinking too much, so I was sworn to secrecy about our destination. I was put into a back room full of barrels and given an orange juice to drink and a book to read, and there I would sit until Grandpa emerged a couple of hours later and a bit worse for wear. His breath smelt like the barrels that had been my recent companions and he was swaying slightly. His speech was oddly slurred but he was mellow and happy. About half way back to the shop he would suddenly announce.

"I'm lost now. Haven't a clue how to get home."

I was thrown into panic and really believed him.

"But Grandpa where do we go?"

"Not sure… what do you think? Left or right?"

And so the game would continue until he would lead us back to the Grove and pretend it was all just a happy coincidence that he found the way.

Grandpa had heart trouble and eventually became so ill that he couldn't look after himself. For the last year or so of his life my Mum took care of him and Grandma at our house. Grandma got quite upset, as she really believed that we would get fed up with her. For me it was a thrill and delight to have them both under our roof. Grandma needed lots of assurance that she was loved and wanted.

When the weather allowed, Grandpa sat out in the back garden on his upright 'director's chair', still as a mountain. The birds would flock round him, unafraid, as he was frail and moved so little. Our yard was a tiny patch of concrete with tufts of grass poking through and a shallow earth border surrounded by wonky bits of grey fluted brick.

"Oh, Linda," he would say. "Make me one of your special cups of hot milk. You know how it makes me feel better."

I loved to help him feel better. It gave me a warm feeling inside. Grandpa's health deteriorated rapidly. Many times I would watch him fall asleep, his now hollow features contorted in pain. He would seem to stop breathing for ages and I would panic, each moment an eternity, until at last he sucked in a tidal wave of air in one long noisy gulp.

I got so close to Grandpa in that final year of his life. One day when I was thirteen years-old I was just getting off the bus from school when I had a really odd feeling. I knew something was wrong. When I returned to Deanery Road there was a note on the front door in Mum's urgent capital letters: GO STRAIGHT ROUND TO LITCHFIELD AVENUE. My heart was pounding. Aunty Mimi told me to sit down.

"Your Grandpa died of a heart attack today."

I wasn't surprised. I had felt it deep inside. I hadn't just lost a Grandfather. I had lost a friend. Grandma only survived one more year before she too passed away. She was taken into hospital with a broken hip and never came out.

We kept all the postcards Grandpa sent from the trenches. In his neat cursive handwriting he wrote regular anniversary and birthday messages and poignant greetings to his young son Colin, and to his adopted daughter Ena. Each card is embossed on the front with tasteful hand embroidered floral designs. On one card that escaped the censor's blue pencil he writes "The place where I bought this card is now in German hands." He desperately missed his wife and children and tried to write letters to them whenever possible.

It must have been agonising for Grandpa to be so far away from his home and family and fighting in such terrible conditions. These cards are a scant record of his life at the time, but they are all that we have. Their impact rests as much on what is left unsaid than the few simple messages they convey.

After Grandma and Grandpa's death Mum tells me what happened to Grandma.

"Your Grandma and Grandpa always wanted another child after Colin, but she didn't conceive until eight years later. Apparently when I was born the sister came into the ward and told Grandma she should call the baby "Mercy". They had discovered a large tumour in her womb, which would certainly have killed her. They performed a hysterectomy by drawing out the womb through her vagina. The operation crippled her for life."

Years later, on Genes Reunited, I unravel part of the tragic truth surrounding Ena. Gerald and I meet up with a long lost relative Lynda and her mother Pat. Pat is in her eighties, the daughter of one of Grandma's brothers. Lynda is around my age. Pat knows all about Ena.

"Your Grandma's sister Fanny married out of the Jewish faith. Disowned by her parents, she went on to have three children – Ena, Elsie, and then Rita. When Fanny's husband died young, Fanny could not cope and committed suicide by apparently drinking cleaning fluid. She died a painful harrowing death. Elsie, as the older child went straight into Service. Your Grandma took in Ena when she was ten, and Arthur Barwell, your Grandma's other brother, adopted Rita. Arthur and his wife Bessie brought up Rita as their own. Ena was never allowed contact with her sister, and knew nothing of the truth."

I manage to make contact with Ena's daughter, Gloria, who tells me that on her deathbed Ena cried out for her sister Rita. Only now do I realise why Grandma never talked much about Ena or the adoption. It must have been so painful for her. It never occurred to me to ask who Ena's mother was. It explains the sad expression on her face in those old photos.

The living space that had seemed so warm and homely when my Grandparents were alive was now a soulless empty shell. Walking into the kitchen sent a cold shudder through me; it was shabby, faded and lifeless. Paint was blistered and peeling in the kitchen. The lino was worn and musty, the sink cracked and yellow. After Mum retired she and uncle rented out the business as a fast food outlet. Though Alters the Grove disappeared in 1986, I can still hear the echoes of Mum's voice: "Maryland 4395" and with eyes closed and concentration I can smell the steam from the pressing, and see Alf's roll-up clinging to his lip, as though it were yesterday.

Rose, Harry, Ena and Colin

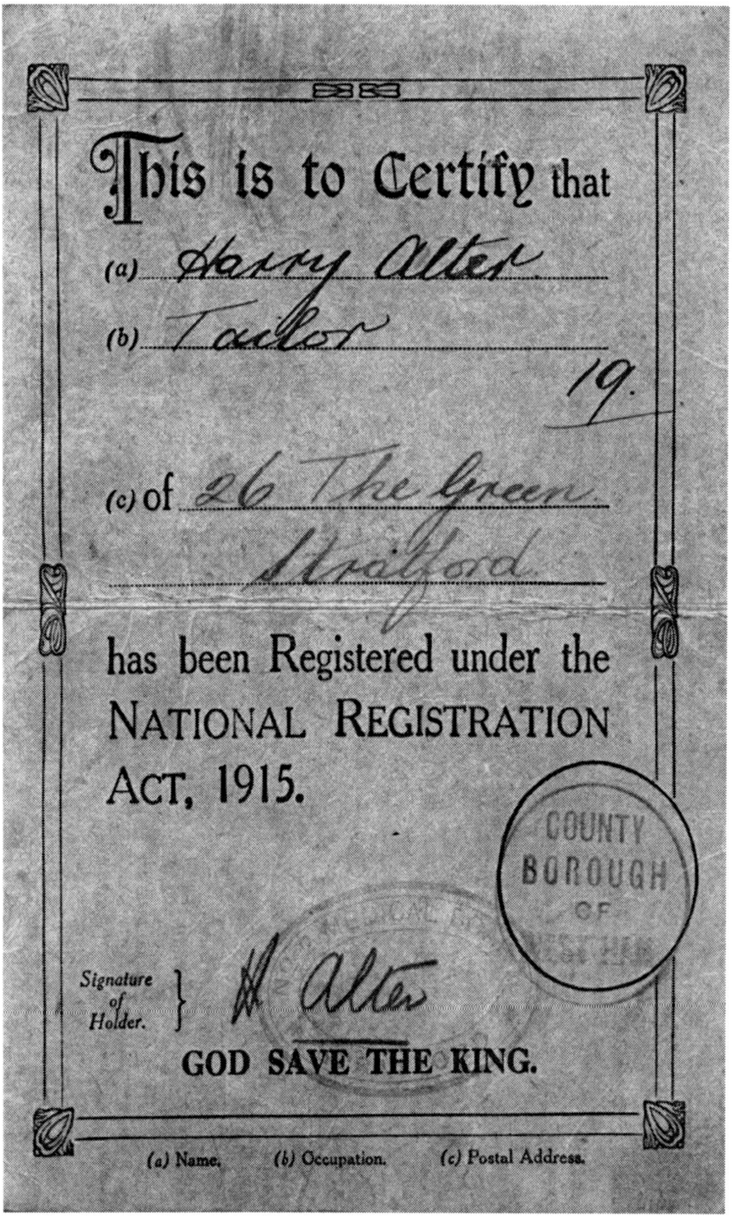

This is to Certify that

(a) Harry Alter

(b) Tailor

19.

(c) of 26 The Green

Stratford

has been Registered under the NATIONAL REGISTRATION ACT, 1915.

COUNTY BOROUGH OF

Signature of Holder. } H Alter

GOD SAVE THE KING.

(a) Name. (b) Occupation. (c) Postal Address.

National Registration – Harry Alter (1915)

Rose and Harry (1913)

First World War postcard fronts

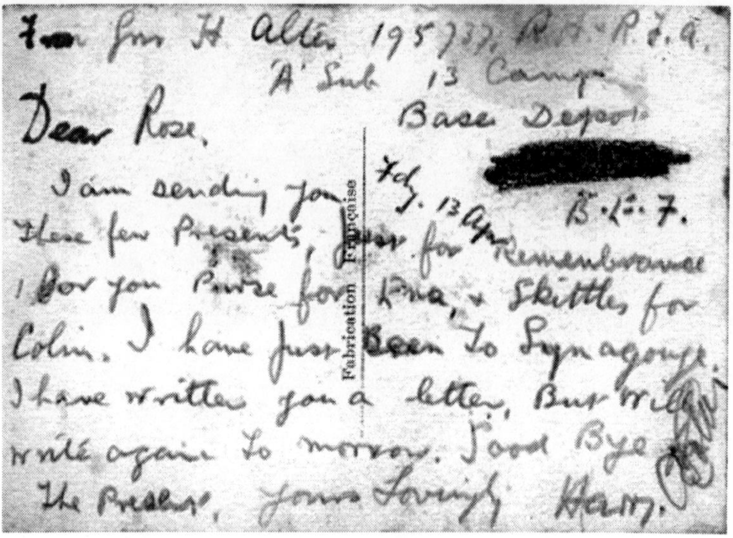

From Gnr H. Alter 195737, R.H.-R.F.A.
'A' Sub 13 Camp
Base Depot
[redacted]
B.E.F.
Feb. 13 Apr

Dear Rose,

I am sending you these few Presents, just for Remembrance 1 Box for you Purse for Eva, + Skittles for Colin. I have just Been to Synagogue. I have written you a letter, But will write again to morrow. Good Bye The Present, Yours Lovingly Harry.

Fabrication Française

First World War postcard from Harry to Rose

Rose, Arthur and Fanny

Gram and me

Gram, Gramps, me, Gerald and Michael

Gram, Gramps, Mum, Dad, Colin, Mimi, Gerald and Michael

Diary – 7th July 2007

The start of the trouble: my first inkling that there was something wrong was on a Sunday evening in early July when I had severe stomach pains. Initially I put it down to colic, but when the pains worsened by morning and I began vomiting I rang the GP surgery. Dr C arrived within half an hour.

"It might be an obstruction, but I can't be sure. Try this anti spasmodic medication, but if there is no improvement you will have to ring back."

As soon as I heard Chris' key in the door I begged him to get me the medication in the hope it would make me feel better. It didn't. By the early hours of Tuesday morning I was writhing in agony. Chris called an ambulance. They admitted me to Whippingham ward in St Mary's Hospital, Newport.

Dr E thought it was a kink in the bowel and he felt sure that keyhole surgery should solve the problem. I had the operation the following day and was discharged by the weekend. I was still on track for my planned trip to Canada to visit my daughter Rachel and grandchildren on July 23rd.

Exactly one week later I don't understand what is happening to me when the pains return, just like before. I am unable to pass anything through my bowel and the spasms are excruciating.

By the early hours I am dehydrated and Chris calls an ambulance once again. This time they are horrid in A&E. The X-ray shows only that I am constipated.

"I am not admitting you with constipation." The surgeon's tone is arrogant and patronising. They send me home after five hours with some suppositories. I spend a miserable day and night in pain until I can stand it no longer. By Sunday I am on the phone to the emergency doctor who advises us to attend the Out of Hours surgery at St Mary's. Hastily we pack a bag. I feel like a freak, more wretched than I can ever remember.

The doctor at the Out of Hours surgery is wonderful. He can see what is happening and makes an accurate diagnosis with no scan and no X -ray. He is on the phone immediately: "I have a young lady with severe abdo' pain. I believe there is a sinister blockage. I want to admit her straight away". I know now that this man saves my life. He takes me round to A&E and ensures there is a bed for me back in Surgical.

This time the doctors are thorough. They send me for a scan and a colonoscopy. Gail, one of the team, comes round to see me shortly afterwards. She draws the curtain round my bed.

"We have seen a narrowing in your colon. We think that the likelihood is the mass is cancerous. Anything benign would not have the same effect."

"No, I don't believe it is cancer," I tell her with the inner certainty that I must be immortal, at least for a few more years.

She won't let it go.

"You need to accept that you probably have cancer. We are going to operate. We will have to open you up this time to remove the mass."

I am gob smacked.

I've had the operation. I open my eyes. "Where am I?"

"You're in Intensive Care. You lost a lot of blood and you needed a transfusion. My name is Ruby. I will be looking after you".

Ruby has soft and tender eyes. She is from the Philippines. She sits at a desk at the foot of my bed. I am full of tubes and drains. It is very peaceful in ICU. There are no other patients near me and few visitors. Everyone has to ring first before they are allowed in. I have a venflo in my neck for all my medication. It feels weird, like I am choking slightly. I am very sick, but Ruby is always there, helping me over it with regular injections. I am able to sleep a little for the first time in weeks. I drift in and out of consciousness. Chris is at my bedside. I can't remember him coming in. When he is no longer there I don't remember him leaving.

I think about my brother Gerald, and his time in the isolation unit back in the Fifites. Few visitors were allowed then. I remember the Sundays I spent with him at Mum's request, because he was so ill.

Life with Gerald

"Oh great. You've landed on Mayfair with a hotel. I make that £1500 you owe me!"

This is Sundays, stuck in Gerald's room again; handing over the brightly coloured Monopoly notes and watching my brother add them to his mounting stash. He wears his purple striped pyjamas and I notice that the pockets are bulging slightly. He's cheating of course; he always does, but I don't argue with Gerald.

My weekly plea of "Mum, it's not fair. I HATE monopoly!" never works.

"I know dear, but you know Gerald is ill," is her stock response.

"He's *always* ill..." But the words, as ever, stay trapped in my head. My mind takes me back to the hospital waiting room. It is a bleak place, its pale green walls and frosted glass doors housing so much sickness and misery. It smells of surgical spirit; Mum has a bottle at home to clean the glass. It makes my head ache. The doctors thought it was meningitis at first, but in the end they reach their diagnosis.

"It's polio," they announce grimly.

I wince, remembering the lumbar puncture and his helpless screams. I feel a deep emptiness and sadness. I sit all alone clinging listlessly to a Rupert Bear Annual, which is supposed to keep me quiet. Everyone has to be quiet. They speak in hushed whispers. They think that Gerald will die. Mum and Dad have to wear plastic aprons and white masks like the Lone Ranger. I'm not allowed in the isolation ward. He'd fallen ill the day that we were due to be immunised at school. Gerald recovered with minor side effects. One of his classmates was not so lucky and ended up in callipers.

The illness hasn't improved his temperament. The mild paralysis in his neck doesn't stop him from surging forward six squares with the tank, while I wait in jail with the 'old boot'. I might hobble on to the Old Kent Road next move, but I doubt it.

"Okay, Linda. Here's the deal. Give me The Strand and the Utilities and we'll call it quits."

"Oh, Gerald. Can't we just agree you've won?"

"Stop moaning and roll the dice. You can write an IOU for the rest."

By the end of our childhood I owed him millions. For some reason, though he knew he could never recoup such a sum, even in play money, he was intensely satisfied. I have never played a game of Monopoly since.

I was fed up being the underdog, being called Ponky (short for Ponkhouse). I never did find out where he got that name. All my birthday gifts would be labelled 'To Ponkhouse', and I hated it.

A few years later I was able to take my revenge. Gerald was used to being waited on, and he wanted me to get him some water. We'd been doing work in English lessons about precise language. I decided to try it out.

"Ok, Gerald. If you can give me an exact description of how to get you your glass of water, I will serve it to you." I ignored his dismissive "Don't be stupid" protests. This time I was determined. Thirsty, and too lazy to fetch it himself he relented.

"Fine. Take a glass from the cupboard. Put it under the tap."

Gerald was not best pleased with the glass of hot water I delivered. Mildly irritated, but very slightly amused, he started again.

"Take a glass. Put it under the COLD tap. Turn the COLD tap on. Now bring me the glass."

Of course I tipped out the water and took him the empty glass.

Mum started to get interested by now, and I saw her face break into a grin. Gerald was looking slightly flushed. His third attempt was going well, until his impatient streak, the shared family gene, kicked in. He had managed to instruct me to fill the glass with cold water. His mistake was in the next five words.

"Now let me have it."

I couldn't resist. It was a moment of pure joy and delight for me. I relished every second. I didn't even get a telling off when I hurled the water at him. I think in that moment my brother developed his first grain of respect for me. It was a long time growing.

It was a terrible winter in 1948 and Gerald was very premature. My Mum had to travel to the hospital every day to see him and bring expressed breast milk to help him survive. He was not expected to live. Having such a poor start in life made him very weak. Aside from the polio he contracted at aged ten, he was hit over the head at Nursery School with a piece of wood that had a rusty nail protruding. The resultant abscess nearly killed him. He grew up quite spoiled with attention and was very demanding. As a young teenager he was a bit of a rebel. My Mum was very worried about him, and wasn't sure how to manage him.

He grew to be strong and handsome in the end, with mid brown eyes and a lovely straight nose. His teachers at school adored him because he had blond hair and looked as though butter wouldn't melt in his mouth. One day on the way to school Mum was explaining that if he was ever on his own he should ask an adult to help him cross the road. Next minute there was no sign of Gerald. When Mum reached the kerb there was Gerald holding some old lady's hand as she guided him to the opposite side of the street. He waitied for us there, with a a huge grin on his face.

We had an open fire in the living room in Deanery Road. One day while Mum was out, Gerald found an almost empty tube of glue and thought it would be a good idea to toss it into the fire and see what would happen. The result was explosive. There was a thunderous roar and a sheet of flame burst into the room, knocking me backwards into Gerald's arms. He was absolutely mortified.

"Linda... Linda... speak to me!"

I am not convinced it was my health that he was concerned about;

just the rollicking my Mum would give him if I'd been hurt. Fortunately there was no harm done. Gerald begged me not to tell. His secret was safe with me and my slightly singed eyebrows.

Gerald was plain mischievous. Mum used to telephone grocery orders from a small local shop called Battles. Mr Battle would pack all the items in a large cardboard box and Gerald or I would run an errand to collect it. Gerald decided it would be a novel idea to phone in a fictitious order from a non existent address, 8 Acorn Road. He used the same address when the truancy officer caught him! Poor Mr Battle. I often wondered how many times he fell for the trick before asking for a telephone conformation.

Gerald once painted his brand new red toy car with a can of black paint he found in the shed. On another occasion poor Mum spent hours scrubbing boot polish out of his ears and from his face. He had found a tin of it and thought it would make good war paint.

I remember he found Grandma's smelling salts and put them under the cat's nose to see how he'd react. I have never seen an animal jump so high. Gerald was going to plaster the cat with vanishing cream too, to see if it would disappear, but was fortunately persuaded not too.

Having friends over could be an embarrassment. Gerald replaced all the custard with salad cream in the custard tarts, and poured out beetroot juice and told my friend's sister Marilyn it was Ribena. Marilyn cried. She never came round our house again.

Diary – 1st August 2007

I have postoperative complications; a narrowing of the lower bowel caused by the surgery. I can't keep anything down, and crave liquid. The paramedics are gentle and kind. They put me on a drip before taking me into A & E, but my tongue is sticking to the roof of my mouth.

In A&E whilst I wait on an uncomfortable trolley to be admitted to the ward I see the staff drink endless cups of juice. I want to mug them to get some. I beg for some really cold water. One nurse promises to fetch me some iced water. I watch her in desperation. I can't move. She disappears and I don't see her again. A doctor brings me some tepid water to sip, but I bring it straight back up and feel ten times worse. It is 1.30am. They take me for an X-ray and a CT scan. I am eventually admitted to a Medical Assessment Unit while they wait for a surgical bed.

The hours pass slowly. I am very sick. They have to change the bed linen twice. I really don't want to go on.

The orderlies offer everyone food and drink. But I am Nil by Mouth.

On this ward there isn't even ice to suck. The staff buzzes round busily. I am desperate to get back to Whippingham ward, where I know the nurses and they know me. The hours pass slowly. I lie here staring at the ceiling. I just don't understand why and what is happening to me. Late afternoon, and I am finally transferred to the ward. They bring me crushed ice and a straw. I can manage only the tiniest sips. Another stomach tube eventually relieves the symptoms and I begin to recover. My first proper drink tastes like nectar. I savour each mouthful. Hot chocolate. I crave the sugary sweetness and the sensation of something in my stomach at last. A day later my first bite of toast lasts ages and is manna from heaven. I remember those shared meals on my annual shopping trips with Mum. It seemed such a natural thing for Mum and daughter to enjoy.

Lyons Corner House

The annual trip up to the West End on the tube from Stratford to Oxford Street brought my birthday to life. Every year as my special treat, Mum and I did the January Sales. Nowadays the very thought of being jostled and pushed around fills me with dread, but oh how I loved it then. We would walk the length Oxford Street, in and out of the superstores, as far as Marble Arch not minding the ever-increasing crowds; it just added to the excitement. We would seek out sale items, usually my birthday present and bonus gifts, like a purse or handbag, a new jumper or skirt. I loved the thrill of the search, the buzz of our fellow bargain hunters. By the time we arrived at Marble Arch we would be ravenous.

"I bet I know where you want lunch!"

"Can we go to Lyons Corner House again?"

Our routine never varied. It was very special to go to the Corner House. The building was art deco style, colourful and bustling, with bright lights and ingenious window displays. Corner Houses were smarter and grander than the local teashops and provided a degree of escapist relaxation. *Maison Lyons* at Marble Arch had a selection of different restaurants. It was my only experience of eating out aside from roadside cafés. We chose the self-service *Braisserie*. The thick dark carpet muffled people's voices. We queued by the plush crimson ropes supported by shiny brass poles as music played softly in the background.

Luxury!

"What do you fancy?"

"Egg mayonnaise and trifle please."

The salad was beautifully presented. The egg sat in the middle of the plate, carefully halved, topped with creamy mayonnaise and decorated with strips of soft sweet pimentos. Mum and I would spend ages savouring the food. Only once did I stray from that meal with a lattice pie. I misjudged a fork move and sent the remains of my desert shooting across the royal blue carpet. Mum thought it was hilarious and had to stifle her giggles.

I was deep fried in embarrassment and thereafter stuck to my very faithful trifle. This was served in a generously sized oval dish with infinite depths to explore. Dipping the spoon in would uncover the hidden delights. First came a thick layer of whipped cream. Just below lurked lush vanilla custard. Further digging uncovered a soft sponge soaked in succulent sherry and fruit juice.

The meal in the Corner House crowned the day. With comfortably full stomachs we would carry all our parcels back to the tube. We were weary on the way back but would chat excitedly about our purchases. Once home we spread them out on the couch and re-lived the experiences.

"That's a lovely jumper; it's really soft... half price too! Didn't we do well?"

"Oh, Mum. This purse looks lovely. What a stunning dark green! The leather feels so soft. Do I look okay in this skirt?"

We continued those annual trips long after I left home and married. The Corner Houses had all closed by 1977. When Brent Cross Shopping Centre was built we went there for a few years and then to Lakeside. The culinary experience was no match for *Maison Lyons*, but the annual outings provided a wonderful bonding between mother and daughter. We never ran out of things to say. It stopped only when Mum became crippled with arthritis and just couldn't walk any distance. She proudly refused to use a wheelchair.

Until then, those excursions highlighted my year.

Diary – 13th August 2007

Back home once more and my regime of eating small but frequent amounts seems to be working. I chew everything at least twenty times. I take no food that passes my lips for granted. I thank God every time my bowel functions normally. I don't feel like the same person any more.

I still find it impossible to believe that I have had a cancer growing inside me for at least a year. I was feeling exhausted, but then everyone at work felt like that. I did wonder why I was breathless just running upstairs, but know now it was the severe anaemia that was undiagnosed.

I find myself going over it all in my head. I am sure that isn't healthy so I try to immerse myself in a book or talk to my friends on the phone, Every now and then I return to that dark place in my head where I don't want to be. I used to be okay with my own thoughts. Now I try to avoid dwelling on all of this.

I still have not heard from the hospital about seeing the Cancer specialist. Part of me feels I should chase this up; part of me wants to ignore it. I always told myself I would never succumb to chemotherapy. My choices are limited. If I choose not to have the treatment I have little more than a year to live. I have to make a sensible decision, though my body doesn't want any further assault.

Reluctantly I telephone Jo, the Colorectal Clinical Nurse Specialist. She promises to co-ordinate an appointment for me. It is likely to be at the beginning of September. Why did I do that?

My brother Gerald and his wife Teresa arrive on Friday to visit me. As the afternoon draws on I start to feel quite ill. I am getting pains in my stomach and don't feel right at all. After nearly two weeks at home I can't believe there are more problems.

We are to have a meal in the restaurant across the road. Gradually as the evening wears on I realise this is not going to settle. I accompany them to the restaurant, make a half-hearted attempt to eat, but just feel worse. I leave Gerald Teresa and Chris in the restaurant and walk home across the green.

I go to bed, but the pains worsen. I lie awake most of the night, hoping the pains will abate, wanting so much to manage this myself.

By the early hours the pain is unbearable and I begin vomiting again. I am desperately thirsty but can't manage even sips of water. We wait until it is light and then Chris calls an ambulance. I have pins and needles all over me. They have to carry me. My blood pressure is very low.

I am upset that this is happening again. I can't bear the powerlessness I feel, and the lack of control over my health. I can't imagine what has triggered this. My regime had seemed so effective. Chris comes with me.

At A&E they take blood and put me on a drip. An X -ray shows that there are still postoperative adhesions causing these problems. The doctor explains that if these episodes continue they may have to snip the adhesions away if they are accessible. I try not to think about it happening again. It is too upsetting. After a couple of hours they take me up to Whippingham ward.

The drip and nil by mouth settle things down during Saturday. By early evening they allow me to drink, and once I can keep fluids down they stop the drip. By Sunday evening I am well enough to return home. By the time we get home I go straight to bed. I am terrified it will happen again. I don't feel sick any more but I sleep with a bucket by the bed just in case.

Monday morning I am feeling better. The pain has lessened. I don't feel sick and can manage food and drink though I am paranoid with each mouthful.

There is a letter on my desk inviting me for an appointment to see the Cancer specialist first thing on Thursday morning. I have mixed feelings. I desperately need to find out what will happen to me and when. Equally I would rather it didn't happen. The second reaction is illogical and naïve, but I can't help myself. The fear is overwhelming.

As a child my fears seemed so very real to me. How much simpler it would be now, if I could just be frightened of spiders, feathers or thunder storms as I was then.

Childhood Fears

My childhood fears were divided into two sorts. The obvious ones, triggered by real events, like thunderstorms spiders and anaesthetics, and the irrational phobias I could never begin to explain.

I understood why I was frightened of spiders. I shared the fear with others and was not ashamed of my vulnerability. In my child world spiders were a dark, silent ugly creepy species, and you didn't always know they were there until they scuttled across the room or touched your skin. Once Mum was doing the ironing and to my horror I observed a giant hairy beast in the corner of the room, looking straight at me, or so I thought.

"Mum, quick, there's a spider!"

I pointed to the offending creature.

"Shhh! Don't say anything. We don't want it to move."

Under her instruction we spent the remainder of the afternoon tiptoeing round in the hope the spider wouldn't hear us. A couple of hours later we realised we had been speaking in whispers. It was a measure of Mum's fear. An irascible spider would have been too much for her to handle.

My husband Chris told me a story, which still sends shivers down my spine. He awoke one morning with a piece of cotton in his mouth, which he assumed was from the duvet cover. He removed it. Minutes later the same thing happened and he extracted the second strand. This went on for a while until he awoke properly to find a very wet three-legged spider on his pillow.

A thoughtlessly stupid primary school teacher instilled my fear of thunderstorms. We were all sitting on the carpet one day and she happened to relate a tale of a man who was walking along the street and was killed by a lightning flash. He had made the mistake of carrying a ten-shilling note in his pocket and the lighting had struck the thin metal strip.

Years later, at a Secondary School sports event I saw one of the teachers struck by lightning. He was holding a starting pistol and we were watching from the sports arena. There was a sudden flash of light and a massive explosion rattled the stadium roof. Everyone screamed in horror and the teacher fell to the ground clutching his wrist. The lightning had struck his wedding ring. He was rushed to hospital, but luckily suffered only minor burns. His rubber trainers saved his life. Even as an adult I continue to be anxious during thunderstorms.

An equally ignorant dentist sparked fear of anaesthetics in me. One of my teeth in my lower jaw was growing crooked because the milk tooth hadn't fallen out naturally. It needed to be extracted, so Mum took me to the dentist. In those days you were automatically given gas to knock you out. The dentist tried to force a metal block between my teeth and pushed a gas mask over my face. I was absolutely terrified and kept my jaw clammed obstinately shut. At that point he flung down the mask and threw me out of his surgery.

"Take this big baby out of here," he barked.

So full of shame and tears I left. I never forgot the incident. Fortunately for me the tooth came out a couple of days later when I hit my mouth on the belt of Mum's coat as I was running to catch up with her.

They gave me gas when I broke my leg at age thirteen. On that occasion Mum was holding my hand as I breathed in the fumes but then I felt her hand slip away and I was aware for what seemed like a long time as I entered into an uncomfortable and frightening tunnel of unconsciousness my head throbbing, ears pounding, and the all pervading nasty sweet smell of the gas and mask. Mum had to take away my foam rubber pillow, as the smell of it was a constant reminder.

Such fears are understandable to me as an adult.

Other childhood fears transcend rationality; my feather phobia was one of them. In one of my earliest memories (I couldn't have been more than three years-old) I am in the living room in Deanery Road. It is a warm summer's day and the sun is streaming in through the large sash windows. The air is thick with a constant stream of dust motes floating around me. The sheer volume and movement of these tiny specks scares me and I begin to cry.

Mummy explains that they won't hurt me, and that we can only see them because of the light. Her reassurances fail to placate me so she wheels me outside in the pram for a sleep. This was probably the start of my revulsion of airborne matter.

I tried so often to understand why feathers scared me. They aren't alive or anything, and they tickle a bit, but they don't hurt you. Mostly they are white and really very pretty. I used to walk along the street telling myself: "You aren't scared of feathers. You are eleven years-old. You shouldn't be scared of feathers."

Then, out of the corner of my eye, there it was. I spied it on the pavement, wafting in the wind; the single feather. I wanted so much to be able to stand there bravely watching, then to walk past it with scarcely a glance and carry on my way. It was not to be. I ran, as though I were being pursued by the worst monster my imagination could conjure. I did not stop until there was a very safe distance between my enemy and me.

It didn't help that my brother chased me endlessly round the house with a feather duster. I would scream until Mum would come running, thinking I was being hurt in some way. No one understood why that feather duster was so scary, not even me.

My daughter Rachel developed a fear of volcanoes following an enforced separation from me when I had a hysterectomy in 1985. She was only nine years-old. My explanation that that there were no volcanoes between our house and Grandma's house made not a jot of difference.

She too suffered at the hands of her brother. We were on holiday together in Tenerife and went up an extinct volcano, Mount Teide. Daniel threatened to set it off by flinging a rock into the hole. Rachel was petrified, her mind closed off to simple reason.

Diary – 21st August 2007

During my last stay in hospital I found a wonderful crochet pattern for a soft toy. It is rather an endearing looking elephant, with a long graceful trunk, floppy ears and four sturdy legs. I find it irresistible, and despite my lack of practice in crochet I decide to give it a try.

When I tell Rachel about the project she thinks her little daughter Ziva will be enthused. She asks me: "Mum, do you remember that soft toy you made for us when we were kids?"

Creative genius

I decided to be the resourceful sort of mother you read about in magazines. The children were to be admirers and beneficiaries of my creative efforts. Since spatial awareness is not one of my strengths, things did not go according to plan. I had the idea of making a cow with some lovely soft material, a little kapok for stuffing and enough enthusiasm to create a herd. Curbing my tendency to be slapdash I carefully cut out the template. Two sides of the cow; quite an achievement for me. My art teacher at school used to look at my efforts with pity, and his comments might rise to: "Good ideas, less successfully carried out," and other such encouraging gems.

I was feeling very proud of myself. Carefully I sewed the two sides of the soft toy together. It was going well, until 10-year-old Rachel pointed out the fatal flaw.

"Mum, I hate to tell you this, but there is something wrong with the cow."

"Nonsense!" I protested, with the confidence of a soft toy connoisseur.

"Well, look at its legs!"

I studied the beast. There was no denying it; where four legs should have been, there were, strangely, only two. I couldn't understand it.

I had put the sides together myself and each had two legs. I knew that two and two made four. What on earth could have gone wrong? I had created a two-legged cow. Even Dolly the sheep managed four legs, despite being cloned.

When Daniel had picked himself up from the floor, and wiped his eyes, his comment was almost encouraging. "Well, Mum, at least you'd never get one like it in the shops."

Our two-legged cow was unique.

I probably should have left the project right there, but somehow my disappointment spurred me on.

"I can sort this out!" I reassured the children. Using the remains of the kapok I fashioned another two legs and stuffed them.

"This should do the trick," I told myself. I noticed the new legs weren't very symmetrical, but my impatience had kicked into gear by then. I needed to prove once and for all that a four-legged cow wasn't beyond my capabilities. When I attached them to the ailing bovine I ended up with a creature Professor Frankenstein would have been proud of. It still lacked its full quota of legs, but with the addition of two pendulous udders attached wonkily underneath by my clumsily inadequate stitching. Not one of my proudest moments!

I'd like to think it was all Mum's fault in 1947, but to quote my son Daniel in 2007: "You can't blame your dead relatives for everything."

Having watched her own mother create mouth watering golden-brown Yorkshire puddings, it was inevitable my Mum would try to replicate that culinary brilliance to impress Dad.

One fateful Sunday as the beef was sizzling in the roasting dish Mum lovingly prepared the ingredients, beating the egg into the milk until it frothed and then adding the exact amount of flour. To the strains of Frank Sinatra playing on the BBC Home Service she carefully poured the thick glossy mixture into the hot fat and returned the dish to the oven. She paused in her efforts to look through the pastel blue window frame to the narrow garden. The wind carelessly swept a few yellowing leaves across the yard. She and Dad retired to the lounge for a pre-dinner sherry. They sat together on the red uncut moquette settee and enjoyed a cigarette watching the smoke as it rose to the nicotine-stained yellowing ceiling. After their pre-dinner sherry, Mum retreated to the scullery whilst Dad stood expectantly at the table, carving knife in hand.

Mum's cries for help signalled to Dad all was not well. "Jimmy, come quick. Something's happened to the Yorkshire pudding!"

When Dad peered into the oven he realised there was a problem. The pudding hadn't merely risen proud of the baking dish, it had migrated through each of the ascendant oven rungs and had expanded in all directions, clinging obstinately to the sides and top. It was well and truly jammed.

Dad looked at Mum quizzically.

"It's like no Yorkshire I've ever seen before." He scratched his head. First he tried gently moving the rungs back and forth, but they would not budge. Then he took the large carving fork and penetrated the centre of the pudding. To Mum's horror she saw that the crispy outer crust concealed nothing but air. Her enormous pudding was entirely hollow. As the joint got colder, she and Dad spent the afternoon hacking away bits of crust until they finally prised out the charred remains. It was the first and last time Mum was to use self-raising flour in her Yorkshires.

Diary – 22nd August 2007

Home again I reflect on my hospital experiences. From time to time when I was well enough to absorb my surroundings I observed some interesting old folk like Mabel. I knew her patter by heart: "Do you know I am eighty-four years-old? The doctors cured my asthma. They removed eighty-four years of snot from my nose. The Government says no one should be in pain."

Mabel was busy scribbling notes to the doctors at all hours of the day or night. She was assertive, cantankerous, demanding and loud – and I knew more about her bogeys than was decent. She was on an efficiency campaign. "Now," she explained to all the nurses that would listen. "The NHS is wasting all its money. Every day an orderly comes to take away our rubbish bags, then another orderly replaces them with a new one. Why can't the same person do both? I shall write to my MP. I was a civil servant you know..." and so it would continue.

Gloria was another. She was in and out of the hospital like a bouncing ball. She was always moaning and complaining about extreme pain, but I don't think the docs could find very much wrong with her. She enjoyed the role of sick person. I hate it. I feel like a frightened five year-old, but the nurses tell me I am very brave.

Night times are the most stressful. The routines never vary. First the staff come round and settle you down for sleep, administering injections, drips, drugs. This is around ten pm. At eleven they rattle round again with the blood pressure machines and thermometers, so if anyone has the misfortune to have fallen asleep they have no chance of staying that way. The lights are dimmed in the ward, but left glaring just outside in the hallway. Then the noises begin. Initially it sounds like coal being shovelled. The nurses' voices echo in the corridors. The man in the room on his own starts shouting out for 'Annie' at full volume. He believes himself to be somewhere else. It goes on for hours, his voice becoming increasingly hysterical. Nurses and auxiliaries are in and out with commodes and bedpans, emptying catheters and changing drips. It's impossible to rest.

It is a relief when the grey dawn light replaces the yellow glare.

I so value being in familiar surroundings now. The stomach problems have completely settled though I am in an unusual amount of pain from the operation site. Whereas before this latest trip to hospital I was walking a little more each day I am now in intense discomfort just hobbling round the house. The whole area burns and pulls. I don't feel like walking. My body just wants to stay in bed. None of the medication touches this. I am concerned and make an appointment to see the GP.

This is more depressing than having cancer. I can't cope with the constant drain on my energy and spirit. I keep wondering why this is going so badly wrong. I do as I am told; I try so hard, yet I feel worse as each day passes. I am seeing Dr B at the hospital tomorrow. How will I cope with Chemo when I can't even manage today without bursting into tears on a regular basis?

It does not augur well. I wish I had more faith in the Health Service.

The NHS

"I don't like dentists" Mum announced firmly."

"That's okay we don't like people," replied the long-suffering dentist. Mum was paranoid about the medical profession, and I suppose influenced my feeling about them.

At age two, my finger was caught in a slamming door chopping through the very tip and causing a nasty injury. I have no memory of the incident, which Mum treated by shoving back the flap of skin and fastening it securely with a bandage for a week, after which it was fine.

Mum rarely resorted to doctors, treating them with contempt, and I was brought up with much the same attitude. Many of my experiences merely added to my mounting evidence that doctors are often playing guessing games with health. A succession of misdiagnoses only served to reinforce my lack of trust. My brother Gerald went to his GP at age thirty-three with a pain in his leg diagnosed as cramp; two weeks later he was rushed into hospital with a Deep Vein Thrombosis and his leg was amputated.

My Infective Hepatitis after a trip to France was initially diagnosed as 'abdominal migraine'. A torn cartilage in my knee was treated ineffectively for three years with anti-inflammatory tablets for water on the knee. No we were not a family who trusted doctors one jot.

The one that still resounds in my memory happened when I was seventeen and on my way home from school:

I struggle to get the key in the door. Crouching by the hall telephone I hold my arm which hangs limply by my side. Awkwardly I dial the number for Mum's work.

It is a huge relief to hear Mum's reassuring voice on the end. She immediately knows something is wrong. "What's the matter?" she asks. "You sound terrible!"

"I don't know," I reply. "I was running along the road when I felt this paralyzing pain in my arm. I can't lift it. I am in absolute agony."

There was no apparent reason for the state I was in. By the time Mum got home from work I could move my arm again, and though it was a bit sore, there was no evidence of what had happened. After several repeat episodes, Mum eventually took me to the GP. He told me I might have growing pains, or indeed – bizarrely – a spare rib. I thought that's what people ate at barbeques.

The incidents became increasingly more frequent. I started Uni at eighteen and during one phenomenally painful incident I took myself to casualty. There they fobbed me off with strong painkillers and suggested I go back to my GP on my return home. Mum was so anxious by this time that she paid for me to see a private specialist. He was very well qualified in orthopaedics, less so in social skills. Brusquely and scarcely looking up from the X- ray he told me I had calcium deposits in the joint and asked me why I hadn't mentioned them. There seemed little point in my telling him I don't have see-through arms.

The specialist said the problem was caused by the shoulder semi-dislocating over a long period of time, which had caused damage to the joint. He gave it a funny-sounding name and told me I needed an operation to clear away the calcium and pull in the tendons to prevent further injury. So it was that in the summer of '69 (whilst Bryan Adams was strumming his first six string 'til his fingers bled) I was admitted to a ward in Brentwood Hospital Essex. It was my first experience of an adult ward and their first experience of such a young patient. The older women were keen to mother me. Fellow-patients Violet and Gladys 'tutted' their way through the days.

"It's okay dearie, don't fret," they assured me. "Now you make sure they operate on the right bit of you. I had a friend once, went in for a leg operation and they did the wrong leg."

They meant well of course, but I was hyped up almost to the point of hysteria the day before my op. It didn't help that the Egyptian doctor attended the patient in the bed next to me, and I overheard what he was saying from behind the curtain.

"Good morning," he greeted the patient. "How are the fingers today?"

"Aww," she exclaimed. "Them's not me fingers, them's me toes."

That was it. I fled to the toilet in tears locking myself in and determined to sit it out until the danger had passed. Minutes later a nurse was knocking on the door. Violet had reported my disappearance.

"Come on, Lin," the nurse urged. "It will be fine. There is nothing to be afraid of."

"But that doctor doesn't even know the difference between fingers and toes. He's not going to operate on me…"

"Yes, that's because in his language they don't distinguish between fingers and toes. They use a word for digits, which apply to both. Don't worry though. They label the limb they are operating on very carefully."

She coaxed me out of the toilet and I went back to the bed. Violet and Gladys shook their heads in sympathy.

Coming round from the anaesthetic next day, I was dreaming I had been bitten by a snake and was trying hard to move my leg, which was extremely painful. I heard the nurses persuading me to lie still. As soon as I was conscious Violet and Gladys were bursting to tell me what happened. Gladys launched the first rally.

"Well they brought you back from theatre, see, and we saw this bloomin' great cage under the bedclothes. So I says to Violet, 'Poor kid. It was her worst fear. She went down for a shoulder operation and they've gorn and cut open her leg,' and Violet shakes her head and we was both real worried about you. So then I calls over the nurse…"

"Yeah," Violet took over: "I says to the nurse, 'ere how come they've gorn and operated on her leg, poor kid? She'll be proper upset. She was meant to 'ave her shoulder done."

Then the nurse starts laughing. "It's normal procedure to put a drip in the ankle so that the patient has one arm free."

They muttered and chuckled about this for days afterwards.

Diary – 24th August 2007

I am thrilled that Rachel, Jonathan and the grandchildren are coming to see me. It is difficult having only sporadic contact with the little ones, as I worry about bonding with them.

I send them small things through the post on a regular basis; stickers, Mr Men *books; anything that I think might interest or fascinate them. I was heartbroken when I missed my annual trip in July. I appreciate the huge effort Rachel and Jonathan are making to fly here with three small children aged five, two and a half and three months. I hate the idea of being a stranger to them.*

I think back to my Other Grandma and hope that the relationship I have with Levana, Ziva and Batsheva will be more loving.

Other Grandma

When I was seven, it seemed perfectly natural for me to refer to my Dad's Mum as 'Other Grandma'. But looking at it now I wonder if she was ever offended? I always felt uncomfortable with Other Grandma, and preferred to spend my time playing with her costume jewellery by myself in the bedroom. Pride of place in the Grandma stakes belonged to my maternal Gram, whom I absolutely adored.

Other Grandma had eight children and I suppose that she just hadn't learnt how to be demonstrative. Her only way of showing love was in the form of mounds of food that I could never eat. Being confronted with such heaped plates full made me uncomfortable. I tolerated Other Grandma, but I couldn't really ever say that I loved her.

Other Grandma was a refugee from Poland. She must have been born around 1897 and came to England after the First World War. She died at around 60 years-old when I was about six.

She wore her hair in a tight bun, was short and had a merry smile. She spoke a lot of Yiddish, especially to the dog, who seemed to understand little else. "*Geh geschwind!*" had the poor hound heading for the door, tail between its legs.

Other Grandma was very small and one day she was going to have a modern 'eye-level' grill fitted to her stove. There was a slight hitch. The man who fitted it for her was at least six feet tall, so the grill was at his eye level and she needed a stepladder to reach it. Other Grandma's eye-level grill became a family joke for many years.

Mum told me the story of meeting Other Grandma for the first time: "Your Dad took me round there and introduced me. I thought she was a bit cold and abrupt. She looked me up and down suspiciously before inviting me in. I was starting to get a really uncomfortable feeling about it. Then it was time for the meal and she started bombarding me with questions. 'Well, do you eat Lochshen at home?' I thought it was a really strange question. 'Yes we do,' I answered shyly. 'Hmm, and what about chicken soup?' I said, 'Of course we eat chicken soup.' 'And do you know what Knedlach are?' Then the mystery was solved." Mum chuckled. "Your Other Grandma didn't think I was Jewish and was testing me out. Once she realised her mistake she warmed to me."

Because Other Grandma died when I was only six I never really formed much of an attachment to her even though Dad took me on regular visits. One particular visit stands out in my mind:

Mum comes into my bedroom and kisses me lightly on my forehead.

"Time to get up, Lindylou!" She always speaks quietly in the mornings so as not to wake our lodger who lives in one of the upstairs bedrooms. Mum helps me with the little white buttons on my liberty bodice then into my dress and my woollen cardigan. "We want you looking nice, 'cos you're going to see your Other Grandma today."

The orange and black linoleum is cold on my feet as we walk down to the stairs and along the passage to the scullery. We have to be quiet because my brother sleeps in the back room downstairs now that the lodger has his old bedroom. I feel sorry for Dora, our lodger. She slurs her speech. Mum says it's because she can't hear properly. She works at the local paint factory as a mixer. Dora is lonely. She doesn't have any children of her own, so once a year I get to go to her firm's Christmas party.

I stand shivering as Mum turns on the Ascot to get hot water to wash my face. I squirm and wriggle away from the flannel. I hate the squishiness, the slight taste of the Palmolive soap on my lips and the soggy wetness that turns cold within seconds.

"Come on, Linda," Mum coaxes. "Ix, mix, trix, and we're done."

I sit down in the kitchen for breakfast. Mum lets me have the top of the milk on my cornflakes. She hasn't lit the fire yet, but the paraffin heater takes the chill off the room. I smell the warm fumes. Makes me think of the paraffin man. He always has a smile and a joke for me as he dispenses his pink liquid.

"Come on, Lindy," Mum urges. "Eat up your crusts, they'll make your hair curl."

I don't particularly want curly hair, but I chew the crusts anyway.

When I've finished my toast, Dad tells me it's time for us to leave. He helps me as I struggle to push my arms into the sleeves of my duffel coat. They keep catching on the threaded elastic, which holds my mittens together. It stops me losing them but I find it embarrassing at school. Dad is taking me on our weekly visit to his mother who lives two bus rides away in a place called Stoke Newington. First we have to walk to Stratford Broadway.

"Morning Jim... little Linda!" The milkman doffs his cap to us calling out as he climbs down from his wagon. I'm allowed to pet his shiny brown horse. I rub the horse's smooth coat; it's steamy breath hot on my hand.

"Dad – why does he have those things over his eyes?"

"They're called blinkers, so the horse doesn't get frightened by the traffic," Dad explains.

I know what traffic is now. When I was very little I used to wonder why there were always noisy coloured machines going up and down the Broadway. I remember how surprised I was to find out that people sat inside them in order to travel from one place to another.

The first bus is an ordinary red double-decker, but I look forward to the rickety old number 178 that we catch at Clapton Common. It takes us all the way to Other Grandma's house. I'm allowed up the winding stairs to the top deck, which is nearly always empty. The bus creaks a lot and has fuzzy itchy material on the seats, which are red with thin green chequered stripes. I pick up a faint smell of leather and polish.

"Fares please!" The conductor walks through the bus in his peaked cap and smart navy uniform.

Dad hands over a three-penny bit. I love the sound the conductor's machine makes as it punches a hole in the small coloured tickets he gives us. I keep mine clutched in my hand until it becomes worn and

Me and Dora, our lodger

soggy. I gaze at the streets below, marvelling at feeling high up and being able to look down on the cars and people below.

We seem to be shaken and jostled for ages before Dad carefully helps me downstairs and off the platform onto the pavement.

The conductor tugs twice on the cord above his head. Ding-ding! And the bus pulls away.

Dad takes large strides and I am nearly running to keep up with him. I recognise Other Grandma's house. It is a massive Victorian building, which has been converted into three flats. Other Grandma lives on the ground floor, Uncle Michael is on the first floor, with Aunty Edna and Uncle Nat on the top. We have to go up three steep steps to the large dark green front door. Each step has small blue and red mosaic tiles. Other Grandma has lots of grandchildren, because she had eight babies to start with.

I wonder if she ever forgave my brother Gerald. I'm told that when he was five years-old he thought it would be fun to bury her silver teaspoons somewhere in the back yard. Despite a communal digging of the whole garden they were never found.

Gerald was born in 1948. Other Grandma had managed to get hold of some apples, which wasn't easy in those post war years. She left them red and shining on the dining table. When she went into the room, to her dismay, she found that there was a small bite in each of the fruits. Gerald stood there grinning.

"Gerald! Why didn't you take just one apple?"

"I wanted to see if they all tasted the same," was his innocent reply.

As soon as Other Grandma opens the door, I know there is something wrong. Her hair is no different; piled in a tight auburn bun, but her face is somehow not the same. Gone is the cheery smile. Instead her cheeks are sunken and she speaks in a way that scares me. Her chin is strangely wobbly. I can't really understand what she is saying, but Dad seems not to notice. I bury my head in Dad's jacket, much to his annoyance.

"All right, Linda," he says. "You stay down here with Other Grandma, while I go upstairs to see Aunty Edna and Uncle Nat.'

I cling hard to his sleeve.

"No Dad, I want to come with you."

He tries to dissuade me.

"You always stay with Other Grandma. You'll be bored with us grown ups talking. What's the matter?"

I can't tell him, but I won't stay with Other Grandma. Irritated he takes me upstairs with him and I have to just sit in the corner and be quiet. I don't mind. To me, at this moment, anything is better than staying downstairs.

After half an hour, Aunty Edna comes over.

"Come on, Linda. You can help me with the washing. You have to be really careful, but I'll show you what to do." She takes me into the back yard where she keeps a wooden wringer. It's on a metal stand, with what look like rolling pins in the middle. She shows me how to turn the handle, but I have to keep my fingers away from the rollers. I watch fascinated as the socks and handkerchiefs, once plump with water, come out flat and stiff when Aunty Edna feeds them through. It takes all my strength to turn the handle, but with her help I begin to get the hang of it.

When it is time to leave, I don't look at Other Grandma. Dad hasn't a clue what is the matter with me. I say very little on the journey back, not living up to my nickname of 'squawky'. I gaze at the moon from the window of the bus. It is covered by a greyish brown curtain of misty cloud.

"So how was your day?" Mum asks on our return.

Dad tells her what happened.

"So, Linda. Tell Mummy. Why didn't you stay with Other Grandma today? She wondered what on earth was wrong with you!"

I hang my head, not really sure how to explain it but Mum coaxes it out of me eventually.

"She's had an accident. All of her teeth have fallen out. I was scared. She spoke funny and I didn't understand her."

Suddenly Mum starts laughing and ruffles my hair affectionately.

"No, her teeth didn't fall out, you soppy date!" she chuckles. "Other Grandma has false teeth. She probably just forgot to put them in this morning!"

Diary – 25th August 2007

The shadow of the impending treatment hangs over me like heavy smog. The more I read about it, the scarier it feels. I'm told that my resistance to infection will be lowered, and that the chemicals will poison my system. I have thrived on being fit and healthy until now. I resent this intrusion. At the same time I know it is the only way I can survive.

As a child there were many times I dreaded walking through the school gates at Maryland Primary. When I think back to my childhood, nothing, not even wicked Miss Shaddick, is as terrifying as the ordeal in front of me now.

Schooldays

Despite its name, there is nothing 'merry' about Maryland Point; my memories of this school fester uncomfortably inside me.

Wanstead Flats, a large expanse of grass and trees, merges suddenly with the High Street, bustling with shops and people. Further along opposite Cartwright's the Chemist sits a large Victorian building, first opened as a Board School in 1879; Maryland Point Primary. The drab grey bricks of this imposing Victorian institution bear witness to decades of thick traffic grime. Large metal railings sealed like the gates of a prison hem in the playground. The school serves the local East London community of West Ham and Stratford.

School in the Fifites bred austerity. Authoritarian teachers whacked you with an exercise book if you spoke out of turn, or made you stand for ages in the corner, with the eyes of the rest of the class searing into the back of your head.

I don't want to go to school tomorrow. I am in serious trouble. It's been raining through lunch and I have Grandma's colossal umbrella with me. When we leave the dining hall some of the boys encourage me to chase them round the playground pretending I am a monster.

We are having a great time. The umbrella resembles a giant bellows, opening and closing with an exhilarating rush of air. The boys whoop and screech. We are all caught up in the excitement. Suddenly the boys run off and I turn to see the black flapping raincoat of crotchety Miss Shaddick, the Deputy Head, as she marches towards me, with her grey sticky out hair and her surly face, lips twisted into sour lines of disapproval.

I cower in her shadow totally deserted by my playmates.

"You are a very naughty girl. You will stop this nonsense at once... do you hear?" She pushes her distorted face right up to mine. Her voice is menacing and ugly.

"If you dare to disobey me I will give you the cane. You won't ever forget it."

As she walks away the boys come out from their hiding places.

Now they are spurring me on.

"Oh, go on. She won't come out any more – it's raining, ain't it?"

Stupidly I believe them. I start the whole chase over again; ten more minutes of fun is brought to a standstill when I am caught in the act.

Miss Shaddick appears as if from nowhere. She is furious at my disobedience. I see the spittle on her face as she barks at me:

"I warned you, Linda Chevin. Tomorrow I'll give you six of the best."

I don't want tomorrow.

"I'm never going to school again," I tell Mum when I get home.

"I'll ring Mr Lewis and tell them not to cane you," Mum assures me. "There must be another punishment they could use."

So Mum persuades me back to Maryland Point. Mum tells me that Mr Lewis won't allow Miss Shaddick to cane me. Grudgingly I go in next day. I must have had a sense of foreboding.

Mum is wrong. As I sit cross-legged in the assembly hall I am summoned from my place into Miss Shaddick's room where Miss Shaddick takes her revenge on me. She brings out the cane, a long thin gnarled instrument from her cupboard. She makes me bend over and pull up my skirt. I am sweating and shaking with fear. She whacks me hard on my upper thigh, leaving a large red mark. She repeats this five more times. With each descent of the cane on my bare flesh she tells me how wicked I am. I can't hold back my tears of humiliation and hurt. I leave her study sizzling with pain and shame. The rest of the class look at me with a mixture of admiration and sympathy. When I go home and tell Mum she complains to the Head. I hear no more about it.

From day one, I have always hated primary school.

The socks feel scratchy and my obstinate feet don't quite fit inside. "Oh, do hurry up, Linlin, or we'll be late!" Mum grabs my hand and I have to break into a run every few minutes to keep up. Mum kisses me goodbye at the school gate. I see swarms of four and five year-olds being tugged through, some crying, some screaming, and a few refusing to budge. I study them curiously. What is the point of crying? I need to find out what it is like first. A tall man strides soldier-like into the playground and blows long and hard on a silver whistle.

"On the second whistle you will line up and file in quietly."

We stand still and wait for the second toot. Obediently we follow him into the building, which smells strongly of fresh varnish. The floor in the large hall shines like a giant toffee-apple ice rink. We sit down and wait to hear our names. I am to be in Miss Jones' class. I have to share a desk with Peter, who smells and has a large hole in the sleeve of his jumper. He uses his arm to wipe his nose; very necessary but not enjoyable to watch. Miss Jones talks for ages about rules we are forbidden to break. There are too many to remember, and I am frightened that I will break some because I forget what they are.

In the corner of the room I can see crates full of small milk bottles. Miss Jones tells us that when she rings the hand bell, we will each be given a bottle and a straw and we have to drink all the milk before going out to play. The milk tastes warm and gloopy. I feel a bit sick afterwards.

We have to line up to go to the dining room at lunchtime. It reeks of wintergreens and carrot. The grated carrot makes me retch, and I hide it under the spoon because the dinner ladies force you to eat everything on the plate. The dessert is even worse: bulbous black prunes swimming in lumpy semolina. I beg someone to eat mine because it is so disgusting. This time I'm lucky. Peter is glad to oblige with a second plateful and I escape this particular torture. In the afternoon it is 'golden time' when we are allowed to pick a toy from a pile in the corner of the room. I have my eye on a tiny clockwork train on a track, but John grabs it out of my hand. I have to make do with a broken doll. Miss Jones tells us we are going to learn something called an alphabet with twenty-six letters.

"When you have learnt the alphabet, children, you will be able to read from *Janet and John*."

I'm terrified. I can't read and John is horrible. Next day I am in the playground crying along with everyone else.

Things are even tougher in the juniors. Maryland has several teachers who seem to hate small children, and are wholly intolerant of everything we do. Miss Ferris and Mrs. Hinman take pride of place in that category.

Miss Ferris sits like a ramrod at the front at a large pedestal desk. She bawls at us if we move or speak. I don't understand why she is a teacher. She certainly despises our class. Her desk set on a plinth separates her from all the pupils. She makes us line up there so she can put her large red crosses on our work with the occasional tick as rare as oyster pearls on the beach. She doesn't like moving round the room. She doesn't like children. Every ten minutes she looks up fiercely eyeballing us at random and demanding silence. When I stand close the spiky bits of beard on her chin and upper lip mesmerize me.

Whenever I look at the board all I see is a blur. I slip further and further behind in class until I am thirty-fourth out of a class of forty... I am so ashamed. Miss Ferris tells me I am Chinese because I write from right to left. We have to dip our pens into the ink holders on the desk. My work is always smudged like soot on the page. My b's and p's come out the wrong way round.

When I am ten years-old, an eye test shows that I am severely short-sighted and I have to wear National Health glasses. It explains why I once had to stop myself posting a letter into a lady with a red dress whom I'd mistaken for a pillar-box. The circular pink frames of my glasses look ugly. The sidepieces cut uncomfortably round my ear, but when I put them on the world seems a different place.

Cracks in the pavement appear, that I never knew existed. Instead of blurred outlines, objects have vibrant colours. I can see bus numbers and recognise people's faces even if they sit on the other side of the room. What a transformation!

There is a curious smell of floor varnish and stale cabbage and I find myself sitting in the schoolroom next to Margery. The walls are of painted green brick and large sash windows looking out onto a bleak concrete playground dominate the room. We are embroidering small mats with different stitches for each of twenty rows. I glance enviously at Marge's. She's almost finished. She lost patience showing me blanket stitch, which I can't master. Mrs. Hinman hates me. She smashes her hand down on my head if I cross my legs, because it's against one of her rules. I keep forgetting.

I'm still on row one: needle in, needle out, endlessly, pointlessly. I can't do this. I find my eyes riveted on Peter. He has two runnels of mucus streaming from his nose. I can't help wondering which one will reach his mouth first. Just as he wipes them both with his sleeve I realise too late that Mrs. Hinman is striding towards me. The surge of fear makes me shake. I see the thick matting of powder on her pale face as the blue eyes bore into me.

"How dare you!" She grabs my arm and drags me to the front. Thirty-seven faces stare at me. "Look, children!" She holds up my mat for the whole class to see. "Linda Chevin hasn't even finished the first row."

I am exposed. I can feel the red to the tips of my ears, my humiliation complete. I am not allowed outside at playtime for two weeks. Mrs. Hinman has no patience with a left-hander.

No one expects me to pass the eleven plus exam and get to Grammar School. Gerald ended up at a Secondary Modern and Mum believes I will too. In protest I speak to Grandma who tells me I just have to prove Mum wrong if that is what I want. I take the eleven plus exam, and to everyone's surprise (except Grandma of course) I pass. I am to start at Stratford Grammar School in Upton Lane in September 1962.

Looking back it seems strange that I would want to be a teacher myself, given how appallingly I was treated by some staff at Maryland. Perhaps it was the fact that the kind and patient teachers stood out so starkly from that evil morass of child haters, that I was determined to emulate them. They made such an impact on my very fragile self-esteem, nurturing me and helping me, particularly when I went to Secondary School.

Diary – 26th August 2007

Rachel, Jonathan and the children arrive tomorrow. I am so relieved that I am finally out of hospital and will be able to enjoy the visit. I hope I will be strong enough to cope. Today Chris and I meander across the causeway and down to the sea. It is a pleasure to see the wading birds foraging in the mud for food. We hear the throbbing sound from three swans as they glide high above us, wings beating in unison. Sunlight dances in the rock pools. Darting fish are just visible beneath the water, rippling the surface. Gentle waves lick the shoreline, then pull back leaving the damp sand glistening like sparkles on a Christmas card.

I breathe in the seaside smells and hear the distant sound of children's voices. St Helens and the Isle of Wight in general is such a beautiful place. It would difficult to find more of a contrast to the area where I was born.

Our House, Our neighbourhood

Stratford is in the East End of London on the Central Line. Between Romford Road, thick with traffic, and Water Lane, a long dark grey streak on the landscape, we come to Deanery Road. We pass the vast World War II bomb-site, a part brick elevation; an old bath is the only clue that this was once a dwelling place. Now it is an unsightly blot on the street. We go past the Bilverstone's three-up-two-down semi and along Deanery Road, round the corner and towards the old Church Hall. It is ten pm and a dinner dance is in full swing. Excited happy voices resound to the boom boom of the music.

Next door, just past the alleyway, is Number 5. A big blue front door leads into an echoey passageway. The front room is on the left, kept spic and span for visitors, with elegant sofa and occasional table. There is a young boy asleep in the drawing room next-door, ousted from his upstairs bedroom by the lodger. As we go further along the deep embossed black and orange linoleum we notice the walk-in pantry on the right, with its wire mesh doors and faint smell of cheese and preserves. Opposite is a cloakroom leading to the back garden.

The sounds from the church hall bounce round the garden and penetrate the upstairs. Dora the lodger sleeps in the back bedroom but she can't hear the music because she has been deaf since childhood. She is allowed a small gas hob in her room where she heats up a can of beans or soup. The stale food smell lingers long after she has eaten. Two steps lead down from there to a large bathroom.

Further along the hall is a little girl's room. It is a warm balmy summer night and she lies there looking at the large blue sash window, willing the music to stop and trying to block the thudding sounds from her head. She knows she won't sleep for at least another hour when she will be once again alone in the silence of the night.

Below her bedroom is the living room. There is a large open fire, now filled with cold ashes, the only remnants from last winter. There is a corner cupboard full of oddments of cups and saucers hanging on slightly crooked hooks. It used to be perfect until someone stood up and knocked it sideways.

The parents are watching *Quatermass* on a compact black-and-white TV. We go through the brown panelled door into the scullery. This is a tiny cooking area with butler sink, cooker and fridge. It overlooks the outside toilet which still bears evidence of 'who-can-pee-highest' competitions on its brown pebbledash walls. It's a no-go area for the little girl, since her Mum's efforts to keep it clean and fresh smelling are a dismal failure.

Underneath this Victorian semi is a dark musty cellar, which is used as part coal-cellar, part-workroom. Black dust has settled on the rough wooden surfaces. The winter shoes and Wellington boots are stored neatly in the corner; they will not be needed until at least November.

We lived at Number 5 Deanery Road. We had to share the

telephone line with our neighbours, the Allerhands. Mum called it a 'party line' but it there wasn't much of a party going on in our house. Mrs Allerhand appeared to commandeer most of the call time. Mum would pick up the phone, hold it out to us, and we would hear Mrs Allerhand's high-pitched voice squawking through the speaker. Mum would turn her eyes up to the ceiling and replace the receiver several times before she could finally access a dialling tone. She found it infinitely frustrating.

When we popped next door from time to time there was always an unfamiliar sour smell in the Allerhands' front room and I squirmed uncomfortably, desperate to return to our house. Ours was a large semi, adjacent to the Church Hall. Dad purchased it originally for £2,500. In 2004 it was valued at £279,000. The stairs faced the front door and were lined with the same thick black and orange linoleum as the passageway. Upstairs were three bedrooms and a large unheated bathroom with an immersion heater. It took at least an hour before the water was hot enough for a bath. In the mornings we would wash in the scullery using the Ascot water heater. Mum and Dad's bedroom at the front of the house was the largest. Mine was roomy, and adjacent to theirs. Two steps led down to the bathroom and the third bedroom overlooking the back garden. For many years our lodger, Dora slept in that back room, while Gerald slept in the drawing room downstairs.

Underneath the house was a large cellar, which Dad used as a workroom. Part of it was separated as a coal shute where the weekly delivery was heaved in from ground level in thick black sacks.

At the corner of Deanery Road, opposite Deanery Road School, which later became Sarah Bonnell High, lived the Bilverstones. Mr Bilverstone was a thin angular man who worked for the Post Office and drove a motorbike with a sidecar. Mrs Bilverstone's square features reflected her practical side. She was a competent cook and homemaker and when I knew her she was busy having children. Janet was the eldest, then Rita, my contemporary, then Edna, Paula and they finally stopped with the longed-for boy, Bryan.

Every birthday and have course there were always a multitude of birthdays, Rita's Mum did us proud with a great spread. There were sausages, bridge rolls, sandwiches, crisps, cakes jelly ice cream, and wonderful games to play. My favourite was pirate ships. We were blindfolded and made to touch and smell strange objects that we were told were eyeballs, or pieces of flesh, and an assortment of ship's gore, but when we removed the scarf we saw that we had been given wet sponge, or a hard-boiled egg to touch.

Upstairs in Rita and Edna's room was a vast array of dolls and teddies. We would play doctors and nurses for hours, bandaging limbs, taking temperatures and making beds. When we tired of that it would be the schoolroom and marking the register. It was fun for me to play at their house, since they were such a large family compared to Gerald and me. The Bilverstones were strict Methodists and completely respected the fact that we were Jewish. Mrs Bilverstone was always careful not to offer me pork sausages, though I could never really explain that I wasn't allowed the beef variety either since they weren't Kosher. I was too polite to say, so merely declined to eat them!

Next to Rita's house was the bomb-site. As a child I accepted these pitted craters as little more than forbidden play areas. One time Gerald ignored the veto and cut his leg badly sliding into the hole.

Near the Grove was Lavender Street. Bernie Winters (the TV comedian popular from the Fifities through to the Seventies) had a house there. It was a row of tiny two-up, two-down terraced houses that hardly looked big enough for families. The houses huddled together in a street that was just wide enough for a car. My friend Margaret Emmings lived in one of the Lavender Street properties. I was about ten years-old and Mum was worried that I was developing a strong cockney accent. Whenever I told her about Margaret she consistently tried to correct my pronunciation: "No dear, not Emmings. Hemmings!"

My protests went unheeded until one day Mum met Margaret's Mum in Stratford Broadway.

"Good afternoon Mrs Hemmings,"

"Hello, Mrs Chevin. She grinned broadly, showing a large gap between her front teeth. "By the way, it's not 'Hemmings', it's 'Emmings'..."

Mum conceded victory to me. It was a rare moment and one to be savoured.

Diary – 30th August 2007

Rachel, Jonathan and the grandchildren arrive in a taxi. They are exhausted, but happy to be here. I go out to greet them and the pleasure of hugging Rachel after so long defies description.

Levana can't wait to show me the letters she has written for me and as we walk through the door her insistence becomes increasingly frantic. "Mummy where are my letters for Grandma? Please find them! I need to give them to her now!" It is excitement and exhaustion speaking. Interpreting the letters is great fun. They are all written to "Migramainglund" *(My* Grandma England*).*

I didn't think it was possible to feel such strong bonds after more than a year of separation. We have a cuddle and Levana tells me she didn't like the aeroplane because she was frightened by the 'mergencies' on the videotape she was shown. Ziva is still asleep in her car chair so we put her in the corner of the room. Eventually I have a chance to hold Batsheva in my arms. She is a tiny miracle and I love her instantly.

Each night I read Levana and Ziva bedtime stories. The second night they don't settle well. I go back upstairs after the story as I can hear Levana sobbing.

"Tell Grandma *why you are crying." The gentleness of my voice soothes the tears immediately, and Levana tells me she wants me to stay with her for a few minutes. I sit a while, but when I leave the room she follows me downstairs. I lead her back to bed and gently explain that she needs to sleep or she won't enjoy all the fun tomorrow. I promise her that if she complies then I will read her more stories the following night.*

Now it is Ziva's turn. She walks into the lounge with her dolly, telling me, "I don't want this dolly in bed with me."

I say gently but firmly, "Fine. Leave it here and go back to bed like a good girl." I am slightly amazed that she takes herself back upstairs without protest.

When I check on them both ten minutes later they are fast asleep. They have tested the waters, and we have no further problems. Rachel is delighted that the girls settle so well and so quickly.

The week passes in a haze of beach trips, blackberry picking, playing, crafts, and endless stories. There are some 'Ziva' moments, where she just can't cope with the frustrations of being a two year-old. But Rachel is a brilliant Mum and takes it all in her stride.

The house is turned upside down. Mealtimes are a chaotic noisy mess. I love every minute.

I think back to my childhood 'rebellion'...

It wasn't serious and it didn't last long, but at ten years-old I certainly stuck my head above the parapet.

Rebellion

"You are not to play with Andrea Richards. I don't want you going round to her house, and I certainly don't want her here!" Mum's decision is final and not open to negotiation. My whingeing protests go unheeded. Without explanation it's a blanket taboo and I am annoyed. I like Andrea and can't see why I shouldn't play with her. I want to make my own decision about Andrea. My first act of rebellion is my defiance of Mum's strict orders.

"Well I am going round there this afternoon, and you can't stop me!" I leave the house slamming the door. I spend the afternoon with Andrea. Nothing awful happens. I don't turn into a monster. This is how I justify my blatant disobedience. Somehow at the time, playing with Andrea seems more important than anything and I'm not bothered about consequences. Only walking back hours later, does my conscience begin to prick and I know I am in deep deep trouble. I start dragging my feet and putting off the moment I dread when I will be confronted by Mum's wrath.

When I finally arrive home Mum is waiting at the door, arms folded, her features etched into a furious scowl.

"How dare you!" She speaks in a quiet voice that is scarier than her full-blown temper. I know I have pushed it too far this time.

I get a severe tongue-lashing.

"That's it, my girl. Up those stairs… no supper for you."

I lie on the bed in misery, feeling a deep injustice in the whole situation, tears welling up inside me, wondering if it was worth it and not quite understanding why Mum is so against one of my friends.

I plot my revenge. I decide I will never venture downstairs again, whilst Mum is in the house. I am beginning to work out how I will sneak down for food when she is at work, and wonder just how many days I could last like this, when I hear her footsteps on the stairs. She opens the door and with a gruff "There you are," she gives me a sandwich. She doesn't talk to me until later the next day. I have to apologise of course, though I still don't see that it is entirely fair.

The following weekend a group of us are supposed to be going to West Ham Park, just to wander around. Mum tells me I have to be back by four pm. We walk along Romford Road into Vicarage Lane and through the Linden Gate. It is a massive park, and fun to explore. We go on the swings, buy ice creams in the café, and stroll aimlessly through the gardens. I am dawdling as usual, and when I look up I can't see any of my friends. I haven't really taken much notice of the way, being too involved in chatting and playing. Now I have the sick realisation that I am completely alone and totally lost. I panic. I walk for what seems like hours, but all the landmarks are unfamiliar and I am more lost than ever. In the end I co me to a park gate, and seeing a 'Parky' (park keeper) there I ask him how to get back to Vicarage Lane. He shakes his head, and my heart sinks.

"This is Portway. You can't get back this from here. You will have to go back through the park. Be quick now. We close in an hour."

He rattles off some directions, but I am so upset and anxious that I can't remember any of them. I am terrified. I long for just one thing I can identify but I recognise nothing. The park keeper doesn't appear to be at all bothered that he has sent a ten year-old girl on her own to walk through West Ham park.

I have no way to contact my Mum or Dad and feel utterly bereft. My heart is thudding hard, and I am shaking with fear. By now it is well after four. It feels to me like I could be wandering round until all the gates close and I am shut in. There aren't many people about, but I ask everyone I see for directions and eventually stumble upon the correct exit. It is a relief to recognise Ham Park road and I am soon back on Vicarage Lane. I run along Romford Road as fast as I can. Mum yells at me.

"What time do you call this?" She just doesn't listen and doesn't understand that I hadn't intended to be late, but that I couldn't help myself. She isn't interested in my story of being lost. She just assumes it is part of my rebelling and to do with the Andrea Richards episode. So I experience another night with no supper.

Eventually Mum comes upstairs and explains:

"I thought something bad had happened to you. I was so worried. I'm sorry I shouted at you. I was so scared it made me cross."

We cuddle and make up.

Diary – 4th September 2007

My grandchildren have been here for a week. I have held my third granddaughter Batsheva for the first time. She is just three months old. Her beautiful dark green eyes gazed trustingly into mine as she laughed and gurgled on my lap. Magic. The children enjoyed the beach. I indulged them with a couple of wet suits so the English summer wasn't too cool for their bodies. Used to swimming pools they both loved the dynamism of the foaming waves and there was much shrieking and laughter, some of it from me.

They all left today and the house seems eerily quiet. I keep finding bits of fuzzy hair, wobbly stick-on eyeballs and sequins, detritus from the craft kits Levana opened on her birthday. Slowly I collect up the toys and replace them in the trunk.

Despite a lot of physical pain I have felt so much better having the children around. They refresh, inspire and invigorate. If a little exhaustion is mixed in, I have no complaints. Rachel went to a lot of trouble to make Levana a beautiful birthday cake with a carefully crafted number five in white royal icing with sprinkles. Levana's initial reaction: "But Mummy, Levana doesn't begin with an 'S'!"

The children interpret their worlds differently. We eat leeks; two-year-old Ziva eats 'lakes'. We take a wrap for our falafel; she wants another 'flapper'. We like poetry; she enjoys 'poem trees' and can do 'tumble-sauts' all by herself. Levana mentions the 'talkie-walkie' that she uses at school.

I reminisce on Daniel and Rachel's early language. He loved the 'sea girls' at the beach, and 'roast beast' for Sunday lunch. He would often want to know if the door was on the 'hatch'. I didn't have the heart to correct him. Rachel was confused with the 'ck' and 't' sounds. She would ask me to undo the 'buttle' on her shoe, and would carry the milk 'bockle' to the front door. Mind you the children weren't the only inventors of unique language. Dad was always very proud to wear his 'Pierre Cardigan' pullover.

As a family we have discussed the harsh reality of the worst scenario, and they are prepared, though we are now all believing that I will survive this. I have to. I feel rejuvenated and I know now that I need to live on. I cannot allow this disease to take over.

At our local Sunday Boot fair I bought Ziva a Grandma Doll. It is knitted, and wearing an old fashioned apron with a brown bun of cable for her hair. Ziva was entranced. The way that she clutched the doll close reminds me of my own childhood favourites and their important role in helping me celebrate family get-togethers.

Dolly Heaven

I love Rosebud. She is large, made of some sort of plaster, has lovely soft blond hair stuck on with glue, and I can dress her with different outfits. One birthday Mum and Dad buy me a wooden washtub and a washboard with corrugated metal. I decide to give Rosebud a bath and wash her dress. Two problems. The wooden washbowl leaks chronically and I am soaked through within seconds. Then Rosebud, clearly not designed to be immersed in water, slowly disintegrates before my eyes. I am devastated as her arm comes away in my hand and her legs break into chunks of soggy clay. The glue in her hair dissolves and she is even balder than when I gave her a perm last year. Mum dries my tears with her special handkerchief and tries to soothe my distress.

"Rosebud is in Dolly Heaven," she assures me.

"But is she alright?" I sniff.

"Yes. Her arms and legs are fine and she is wearing a lovely new red dress."

I so much want to believe Mum, but I am broken-hearted at the loss of my favourite dolly companion.

To compensate Grandma buys me a doll that cries when you turn her upside down. Although I am grateful to Grandma and try to love

Rosebud mark two, I am disturbed to find a small speaker with holes underneath her dress and am unable to see this strange creature as a replacement for my precious newly-deceased dolly. Another much smaller doll eventually becomes my favourite. Rosebud three is made of a beautiful soft rubbery material. She has chubby pink cheeks and you can bath her without problems and comb and set her hair, which is silken and thick. I spend a wonderful year with her until Gerald decides to draw on one of her cheeks with a ballpoint pen and I bawl my eyes out. I try washing it off, but that doesn't work. In the end I attempt to chisel out the unsightly marks with a knife. My amateur attempts at plastic surgery leave Rosebud irretrievably disfigured but still a great dolly. I try not to notice her scars. On special days (ie when we have a visit from Grandma, which is rare, because Grandma can't walk) I lay out Rosebud's clothes for the occasion and dress her lovingly.

Christmas follows a set routine. We have to wait until after breakfast before we get a visit from Father Christmas.

"Ho Ho Ho! What have we here…?"

He is dressed in a large red robe and wears a white beard. Gerald and I are convinced he is the real thing until we find the costume stuffed in our parent's room one day. Gerald swears me to secrecy so that the fun can continue year on year. He gets his presents and takes them to pieces to find out how they work. This usually damages them beyond repair. He then uses them as bargaining chips.

"Right I'll swap you my cash till for your cooker."

I naively agree only to find the till doesn't work. When we ultimately swap back, to my dismay, nor does the cooker. The fancy light no longer comes on when you open the oven door, and the catch doesn't fasten properly.

Then come the Christmas annuals. Gerald gets to read the Superman annual first, while I make do with Beano and Dandy. We are quietly reading the whole morning. The excitement of Grandma's arrival is the highlight of the morning, followed by Christmas lunch round the table. Gerald sets up the Grundig reel-to-reel tape recorder and conducts the interviews.

"What was your favourite part of the meal Grandma?"

"Oh," says Grandma in her rich deep voice. "I liked the way the potatoes were peeled." She would make a positive comment about any part of the meal that she knew I had helped with.

Gerald's sweet unbroken voice would list all his favourite presents. "From Grandma and Grandpa I got a new pair of pyjamas. From Mummy and Daddy I got a racing car. From Linda I got a game of draughts."

We would sing a few songs and while the grown ups slept off the excesses we would play with our toys. Bliss.

Even after Grandma and Grandma died, Christmas was a great excuse for a family get-together. Rachel and Daniel had a wonderful relationship with Mum. We played endless games together which gave us all immeasurable fun. Mum had a heart of gold and loved us all very dearly. Her unparalleled good nature and generosity subdued any competitive desires she may have had, so playing games with her was always amusing. Mum was the peacemaker and wanted everyone to be happy. The game that made a special appearance throughout the Eighties was called Colditz.

Colditz Castle was the fortress deep in Germany, which held captive the very best escapers of World War II. One player takes the part of the camp security officer, while the others play the 'Escape Officers' who are responsible for organizing escape attempts by their teams of prisoners. Generally, the winner will be the Escape Officer who achieves the most successful escapes; but it might be the commandant if he can limit the number of escapes.

Playing this board game with Mum was somewhat challenging, because Mum would always volunteer to be camp security officer. This was not, as you might imagine, supporting the aim of the game by preventing escapes, but so that she could show her love for her children and grandchildren by benevolently allowing us to acquire enough equipment to run away.

"It's okay," she would assure us in her loving way. "You can take the wire cutters. I'll position my men away from the gates so you can break out tonight."

"But, Mum!" we would protest. "You have to toughen up. You are supposed to STOP the escape attempts, not encourage them. What are you thinking?"

"I don't mind though."

Mum wanted a happy contented family. She was happy to lose. The children absolutely loved it; they won every time.

Mum kept us entertained with anecdotes from our family archives too. We often asked for the same stories over and over again. A favourite of ours was her encounter with a lion at the circus. Mum's eyes would glaze as she reminisced over that fateful day at Wanstead Flats.

"When Gerald was five, I took him and your cousin Michael to Billy Smart's Circus. It was a very special treat and I managed to get ringside seats. Both boys were really excited, and sat either side of me. Their mouths were agape all through the flying trapeze artists' act, and they shrieked in all the right places when the clowns performed their slapstick routine. Then came the lions. You should have seen Gerald and Michael! Their eyes were like saucers. We were really close to the arena. The trainer got one of the lionesses to jump up on its box. I saw this massive beast lift its tail and before I could move, a huge jet of wee-wee propelled itself right into my lap. It spurted out like a full-on garden hose. I didn't think it was ever going to stop. It must have been at least a bucketful."

When we'd reacted with sufficient "Oh, yeuk! That's disgusting," type comments, Mum continued the tale.

"Of course it was the best bit of the day for Gerald and Michael. They were under the seats with laughter. The rest of the audience found it a hoot too. I absolutely reeked. On the journey back no one would come anywhere near me. I have never been so embarrassed. Trust me, I never sat at the front near the arena ever again, and don't you ever mention the word 'circus' to Gerald or Michael!"

Gerald and Michael had been quite a pair in those days. Uncle Colin, Aunty Mimi and Michael lived close by, and one day Gerald rigged his own microphone system with wires across the back garden so he could speak to Michael whenever he wanted. He kept an earpiece under his pillow and they buzzed each other regularly.

They soon expanded the idea into their own radio station called 'Wham' until the neighbours complained about the overhanging wires, and the GPO who ran the telephones in those days insisted it all got taken down.

Once Gerald and Michael put a 'broadcast' of their voices into our radiogram in the front room, and Mum jumped out of her skin when she was cooking Sunday lunch because disembodied voices boomed out in the living room.

Diary – 6th September 2007

The Registrar tells me that they will probably operate on my liver following a discussion with the surgeons, but they need more detailed scans in Southampton to determine the size of the tumours and to decide if chemotherapy should be prior to, or after, the operation. I am to wait two or three weeks for these.

I ask if a few more weeks will make any difference to my chances. The registrar shakes his head. I have to play a waiting game now. I am relieved that the chemo is not to start straight away. At the same time I am worried that this treatment will drag on and on.

There is a trial drug not available on the NHS. If I agree to be part of the trial, then I have access to this possible cancer shrinking drug as well as chemotherapy. One of the side effects is a skin rash akin to acne. It will affect my looks. I have never been particularly vain, but am not sure that I want to be transported back to some of the seedier sides of being an adolescent. I struggled enough at the time.

Lamb dressed as Mutton

Age is a privilege. You can dress as you want, wear your hair short or long at will, and for me at least the best bit is just being comfortable.

At age 13, life was not so simple. There was overwhelming pressure to conform. I was a bit of a Tom Boy. I couldn't be bothered with girlie stuff and just wanted to have fun, run about, and be a kid. It took some courage to be like that and avoid the lifestyle adopted by my friends; they liked 'dressing up' in pretty frocks, but for me it was shorts and a t-shirt in summer, slacks and jumpers in winter. One day we decided to go and see an X rated film *Curse of the Mummy's Tomb* at the Rex. It was supposed to be terrifying.

My friends scrutinised my cardigan and slacks. "Oh Linda!" they despaired. "You look about ten! Right, we're gonna make you look sixteen. It's only the local flea-pit. It's so dark and dingy in there they won't look that closely… ready?"

I grudgingly accepted the invitation to dress up.

The transformation took about half an hour. Lynne held the disgustingly red lipstick and tried to apply it to my unwilling lips.

"Come on, keep still," she said. "It won't take a minute."

"But it tastes foul."

"Don't make a fuss now. Just purse your lips. Good. Jessica, have you got the suspender belt?"

Jessica passed across the most clumsily uncomfortable piece of clothing I have ever put on. The clips bit into my thighs, the stockings imprisoned my legs.

"Stop scratching like that!" snapped Jessica.

"But they are so itchy…. can't I just wear socks?" I protested weakly.

They ignored me. Grudgingly I squeezed myself into the tight skirt and slipped on the high heels that pinched my toes. To add to these indignities, Lynne started backcombing my hair and as I squirmed she sprayed on a lacquer, which felt like a glue fixative and smelt even worse. It was utter misery.

"Let's have a look at you then…"

I walked up and down awkwardly.

"Hmm. You'll do I suppose."

So it was, that dolled up to the nines but still looking like a ten year-old with lipstick, I passed the scrutiny of the lady at the desk, who appeared mildly suspicious but not particularly bothered. I don't remember much about the film. The music was creepy, the Mummy of the centuries-dead prince less so, as he rose unconvincingly from his sarcophagus and began robotically patrolling his new London surroundings. I knew just how he felt.

The bit I remember most vividly was spending the whole film picking at a thread on the knee of my stocking and ending up with a satisfying hole through which at least my kneecap found freedom.

I look at myself in the mirror today. My hair is cropped; I wear a comfy pair of cargo trousers with a casual shirt. The lady at the Rex, if it still existed, would let me in just as I am.

The freedom to be me is a joy.

Stratford Grammar School (SGS)

I feel like a tailor's dummy, stiff and odd encased in my white shirt, purple and navy tie, eight gore skirt that Dad made for me on the sewing machine last week, itchy navy blazer with the smart SGS badge and worst of all this – a beret that looks weird at every conceivable angle.

I am a first year. As I walk self-consciously to the bus stop in Romford Road to catch the 278, which will drop me at Upton Lane, I hear some children shouting at me "Grammar Bug!" It isn't nice to be called names, but I am used to this sort of nastiness, and besides I am proud of my achievement. I passed my eleven plus exam. I deserve to be at Grammar School.

I get off just outside the Spotted Dog pub at the corner. I have practised the journey during the holiday, so it feels fairly familiar. Nervously I walk towards my new school. I glance up at the modern Sixties building. It stands on several floors, encased with windows, each floor depicted in coloured concrete. I am proud to go into the playground. It is a stark contrast to the dilapidated Victorian primary at Maryland.

Still feeling at odds with this beret perched jauntily on my straight dark hair I wait with a bunch of others. It is easy enough to make friends. I meet Val, Lynne Marilyn and Evelyn. We are all nervous, laughing at our berets, wondering what the day will bring. By the end of day one it is clear that the berets are removed the moment we are out of sight of the school building. Marilyn says so, and we all learn to listen to Marilyn.

Initially I am frightened the work will be too hard. My memories of puzzling over long division in Maryland still haunt me. "Divide three pounds nine shillings and three pence three farthings by two and tuppence ha'penny". My number work was so messy, never stayed in columns and my answers were always wrong.

Grammar School seems a lot easier to me. Mr Punshon is my favourite teacher in those first few weeks. He makes the whole class laugh and brings History alive. He allots all the students in the class historical roles in the settings he describes. Young Stewart is the baker in Pudding Lane who starts the fire of London. We picture him in his white hat kneading bread dough.

I don't get in trouble for misbehaving or talking in class in those early years, but my absent-mindedness earns me my first and last ever detention. We are supposed to get our reports signed by both parents and return them on the first day of the following term. Mum and Dad leave for work early, so I just forget. This slip up leads to my first punishment. I am petrified of having 'detention', not really understanding what it means.

"Mum, I am scared of going to school tomorrow because I have a detention."

Mum reassures me. "Remember, anticipation is always worse than realisation. Just go in and do it. You'll feel better when it's over."

I take her advice and it is nowhere near as awful as I feared. I am just told to sit in a room after school with some other students and to copy out some work. I have to say the sanction did nothing to improve my memory, but it honed my skills in forging Dad's signature for future occasions. Looking back it does seem harsh. But in the Sixties, staff were strict and you followed instructions.

Before SGS I never realised school was a place where you could laugh and be happy. I remember being relieved at Maryland when my annual bout of tonsillitis kept me in bed for two weeks. I wouldn't have to go to school. When they finally took my tonsils out in 1961 it was great; though I was very ill I got a whole month off school. SGS gives me confidence. I am no longer thirty-fourth in a class of forty.

I am below average in Maths and Geography. Science isn't my

strongest subject and I am not sure that our Chemistry teacher likes me very much. Asked in a test "How do you remove permanent hardness of water?" I respond: "You can't remove it because it's permanent." I wasn't being cheeky. I didn't have a clue. Similarly my Needlework tutor is not impressed, given that my Dad is a tailor. I spend a whole term making a skirt, but end up getting carried away.

The teacher holds up my finished garment. "Well?" she challenges.

I look at my carefully worked seams.

"It looks straight to me," I offer timidly.

"It may be straight Linda, but would you like to tell me how you are supposed to step into it?"

In my enthusiasm I have managed to sew the bottom two hems together.

I do reasonably well in History and excel in English and French.

One of my poems is read out in assembly. Mrs Phillips says it was the best one from the whole class.

The title we were given was *Starving Child:*

Starving child? Can't spare a thought,
Gorging myself on the sweets I bought.
Voices pleading: "Give some money, please help the fight
To ease the burden of a poor child's plight."
I would donate, for I'm not mean,
But my money is feeding a slot machine.
Get that rocket to the moon!
More worthwhile than to fill a spoon
With food
For a starving child. Besides, he'll survive.
Starving child? Hear the poor thing's died.
Never mind. No disgrace.
There's plenty more to take his place.

Finally there are subjects I am good at!

In PE I am not great and my teacher hasn't much time for me. I am shunned in Netball, since I can neither run fast, catch a ball nor score goals. One day in my second year we are trampolining, and I am paired up with another girl. It is going reasonably well until we get out of synch. As I come down, the trampoline comes up. I feel an awful pain in my leg and hear a loud crack in my ear. Everything goes black for a moment. I realise I have probably broken my leg.

The teacher doesn't believe me and makes me try to walk. Somehow they get me to the medical room and ring my Mum. They see I am genuinely hurt and eventually call an ambulance. I have broken my leg in two places (tibia and fibula) and have to wear a cast for six weeks.

Mum rigs up a tin bath for me downstairs, which she carefully fills with kettles of water. As I lower myself in, plastered leg hanging over the side I realise the water is too hot. My cries of "Ow, quick get me out!" are just met with another spasm of Mum's hysterical laughter. Much as she wants to rescue me from my plight, she is helpless with giggles. Mum's laugh, as always, is infectious and I end up joining in, suffering nothing worse than a red bottom, and a marginal loss of dignity.

By the time I make it back to school the rumours are rife: I have dislocated my shoulder and cracked my skull. Of course we could sue the school but Mum thinks that would put us in a bad light so we let the matter go. My PE teacher is a lot nicer to me on my return.

In my third year I learn Hockey. Mrs Phillips, my favourite English teacher coaches the team. I take to it like a natural and work my way up as Right Half into the Second Eleven team. I go to away matches. I learn to like myself a bit. I even get picked twice for the First Eleven team. I am a strong swimmer too and others want me in their relay. I have never been this happy. Not even Mrs Punshon's sarcasm can dampen my spirit. She is strict and asks us to bring in a book we are reading.

Mine is a fantasy book on time travel, set in Edinburgh. She picks it up and sarcastically says: "I didn't know you liked Scottish books."

I flush red. Years later I realise what a ridiculous statement that was. She was power mad. Even at secondary school there are teachers like that, but most are wonderful and I really admire them. I want to emulate them too, and decide early on that I want to be a teacher. I make a vow with myself never to humiliate a student because they have a learning difficulty. In thirty years of teaching I have stayed faithful to that early promise.

A trip to Paris in 1965 is great fun. It costs £30 for a week. We stay in the Lycée St Louis on the Boulevard St Michel. It is a boys' grammar school and the toilet facilities are basic even by French standards. Evelyn is vocal in her response to her first visit to the loo. "I ain't goin' in there," she announces with a finality that leaves us in no doubt as to her feelings on the matter. "It's an 'ole."

Sure enough she is right. It is a tiny cubicle with a hole either side of which are two foot pedals. This was clearly not designed for females. You are supposed to crouch with your feet on the pedals. Problem comes when you flush. If you don't jump out of the way in

The 'ole

time you end up with your feet in a cascade of sewage water.

We found ourselves having to cross our legs until we got to the Alliance Française for our daily lessons. Not easy, but worth the inconvenience.

Paris opens my horizons. I find it exciting, colourful, and beautifully different and a great opportunity to practise my ever-improving language skills. We meet up with some lads. Mine is called Leo. He tries to chat me up by whispering sweet nothings in my ear, but to his dismay I am only interested in practising my French. The desire to be a language teacher burns on within me and lasts to the end of my time in the Sixth Form.

In Lower Sixth I do a crash course in Latin, which I need if I am to go to University. Mr Myers is a total eccentric. He came from a private boys-only school and isn't used to girls at all. His straw coloured hair is crudely hacked into a short back and sides. He always wears a billowing graduate gown, which engulfs us with chalk dust whenever he marches and twirls around the room. He bellows at tables and chairs to demonstrate the 'ablative' case. Front row students have to duck to avoid his spittle. If we don't answer him immediately he taps one foot impatiently: "Well come on, what is it? Pussy? Pussy?" which has all of us in hysterics. I pass with a good grade. I am so proud.

In French I generally come first or second in the class. For some reason it all stays in my head. I go on to do A-levels in German, French and English. I don't like Mr Greenstein. If you get a word wrong in a test you write it out ten times. Two words twenty times each. I don't learn well that way. I much prefer Mrs Dethan. She is easy going and likes her students. Some mess her around, but those of us who want to work sit at the front and she nurtures us with her expertise. I got my grade one GCE thanks to her.

Mum and Dad drop the bombshell in my fifth year at SGS. They can't cope with our neighbour's all night parties and the weddings next door in the Church Hall that go on until late at night every weekend now.

"We are moving house. This area in Stratford is too rough. We are going to Barkingside."

"But how will I get to school?"

"You'll be able to catch two buses. It won't be so bad. It's only for a couple more years"

"It's not fair. I love this house. I don't want to move."

My moaning and bleating achieves nothing of course. The first house my parents look at falls through because they discover dry rot. The second attempt is 95 Ardwell Avenue. It has a large narrow garden, which they love, two reception rooms and three bedrooms. The problem is that I am to have the 'box' room, with barely enough space for a bed. No desk. I will have to do my homework curled up by the windowsill. Gerald gets the bigger room because he is older. I think that is grossly unfair, but that's the way it is.

The other problem is that we have to sell Deanery Road to Queen Mary's Hospital Housing Department and move out before we can get to the new house. As a result we spend a miserable six weeks living above my grandparents' shop in the Grove. It has been uninhabited for three years following their deaths. It is smelly, dingy, cramped and disgusting. I have to sleep on a camp bed in the vast bathroom. There is no running hot water other than an immersion heater that takes forever. The bath is horrible and full of spiders. I am adjacent to the 'old room', which has no windows.

I am waiting for my GCE results and the tension is palpable. We are always arguing. I am so rude one day that I get a slap round the face from Mum. It is the last time she ever strikes me. I know I deserve it. I just pushed her too far. Part of me longs for the boundaries still to be there. I am sixteen but there is still a frightened child inside me.

Diary – 10th September 2007

They bring forward my postoperative check up.

I tell the doctor my concerns about the time delay. He says that he will try to speed up the scans. He encourages me to move as freely as I can in the interim and do what I want, now that we are more than six weeks from the operation.

With some trepidation I go down to the sea for my first swim since the obstruction. I walk into the water, and feel the coldness creep up my body. It is a beautiful sunny day so I just relax into smooth even strokes, head aligned with body, perfect unison as I carve my way through the still water. The enjoyment is immense. There is no pain now that my body is supported. The salt feels great against my skin.

The whole experience is soothing. I am at one with this element and give thanks that even for just a few more days or weeks I can do this.

Southend-on-Sea

Dad flings open the living room door, a big grin on his face, hardly able to contain himself:

"Frances, I have something to show you. Come and see!"

"I'm busy, Jimmy. I'll look later. My hands are dirty, I need to finish peeling the potatoes."

"The potatoes can wait. You'll love this. Come on Gerald, Linda, lets go out and look."

Mum ambles down the long passage, muttering to herself and we trail along behind, wondering what all the fuss is about. At the street door, our mouths drop open. There in the kerb, parked askew but all shiny and blue stands a Ford Popular motorcar. Dad can't wait to show it off to us.

Mum is really excited. She is bursting with questions.

"Does it go? Can you drive it? Is it ours?"

"Yes, it's ours. Of course I can drive it," Dad boasts.

We clamber inside. It smells of a mixture of oil and leather. Dad pulls out the starter, and after a few coughs and stutters the engine springs into life. We realise Dad has greatly over-estimated his driving prowess as we perform kangaroo hops along the length of Deanery Road while Dad practises on something called a clutch. Gerald gets out and starts running up the road faster than Dad can drive, shouting and gesticulating.

For once Dad doesn't get angry at his antics. I've never seen Dad look so proud. What a thrill. Mum and Dad discuss something called HP, which isn't the brown sauce Dad puts on his chips.

We are a mobile family. As Mum and Dad both get used to driving,

Gerald and the Ford Popular

we take regular weekend trips to Southend in the summer months. It is thirty miles away along the A12 but to us it is as exotic as a trip abroad. We count the roundabouts, look out for familiar landmarks and play games with number plates to see who can find the funniest.

As we approach the Half Way House pub, excitement mounts. We cheer at our first glimpse of the sea!

At the beach in Chalkwell, we start unloading. There are deckchairs, buckets and spades, drinks and a picnic. Some weeks Dad treats us all to hot pasties or sausage rolls in the kosher pie shop. The pastry is golden and crumbly.

It is always exciting when the tide is up, but Southend is renowned for tides that go out for miles. Gerald and I like to wade out on the mud flats. There we can spend time exploring the rock pools and watching with fascination as the winkles open trustingly, exposing slimy fat bodies protruding from shells, antennae outstretched onto our bare palms. One touch of the finger and they spring back, clamming shut in an instant. It provides us with hours of fun. One time I am carried away watching a crab scurrying just beneath the surface and begin burrowing into the wet sand, when Gerald grabs my arm.

"Quick… we have to go. Hurry up!" He starts dragging me back.

"Wait! Wait! My paddler is coming off, I can't walk."

The mud is really deep and I struggle to lift my feet. Gerald takes no notice of my squealing protests.

"We have to go now. There isn't time. The tide is coming in."

I look up at Gerald's face, contorted with anger and fear, and realise he is serious. The water is encroaching on our patch of mud from all sides. My paddler sinks into the ever-softening sludge and I try to retrieve it, but Gerald yanks my arm. By now I am stumbling and crying, sensing his fear, but not really understanding the implications. I am being half dragged in the thick gloopy mire, when a figure clad in shorts and a sleeveless vest comes hurrying towards us. I notice with relief it is Dad. He is very cross, picks us up, one under each arm and sprints towards the beach. Only once we are back with Mum do I realise how close we came to a tragedy. We had walked out too far on an incoming tide.

Sometimes Dad takes us to Chalkwell on a Saturday when Mum is working. He gives us ten shillings to buy himself some afternoon peace. We can use it for lunch and to have a go on the amusements at Southend. Gerald walks me up to the Kursaal fairground, where we buy hot fish-and-chips wrapped in newspaper.

As we munch the succulent chips and crunch our way through battered cod, we wander round deciding how to spend our money. We start with the Dodgems which is always fun. Gerald doesn't do dodging, so we mostly slam into other cars and the sides of the rink, teeth jarring in our heads.

The Scenic Railway is the most thrilling ride. We are strapped into the car, the attendant raises his arm and we are on our way. Anticipation mounts as the carriage slowly jerks upwards higher and higher until we reach the first peak. Without warning we suddenly plunge down at top speed with a stomach churning rush of adrenalin, until we level out and the cycle begins again. Excitement mounts as the peaks become ever higher and the speeds faster.

I always enjoy the Ghost Train. It is creepily dark as we enter the tunnel. After a few seconds a skeleton, lit eerily with a green light, leers right in our faces. Gerald tries his best not to jump out of his skin. I just scream. We feel things hanging down from above that tickle our hair and our faces as we go by. The terror is worse because you can't see what has touched you. Then come the sounds, howling and shrieking at us in the blackness. No matter how many times I do the ride, it never fails to spook me.

The helter -skelter is free. You get a hairy mat and a fast and furious ride down the slide that scorches your legs if you don't tuck them in. Back home in Stratford our only slide is the local coal shute, which we are strictly forbidden to play on. We use it all the time, but the tell-tale black grime on our clothes and hands is a dead giveaway and leads to much remonstration. I never remember it putting us off. The urge to have fun greatly exceeds the fear of punishment!

Late on Sunday we pack up to drive home. We take a detour down a long country road called St Mary's Lane, which twists and winds through the Essex countryside. For us, coming from concrete Stratford, it is an enriching experience to see miles of fields, grass and trees. Half way along is a little café called The Nook. We stop there for tea. Everything is freshly cooked to order and the smells tantalise the palate. I always choose mushrooms on toast. The toast is thick hot and buttery, and the mushrooms large dark and fleshy with a mouth-watering depth of flavour. I have eaten in expensive restaurants since, but have never tasted mushrooms to equal them; today's are insipid in comparison.

Me, Dad and Gerald at the seaside (1960)

After tea we go back along the A12. I am bursting to go to the toilet. Mum stops the car near some bushes. Unfortunately I relieve myself in a bed of nettles. I climb back into the car, face red with embarrassment and bum red from the nettles. Gerald thinks it's a great joke and makes fun of me all the way home.

I hate getting back to Deanery Road. The passageway smells faintly of cat wee and I have school again tomorrow. Yeuk.

Diary – 15th September 2007

It is Chris' birthday today and we go to our local restaurant for a meal. It is a delight to eat food without feeling sick and I am able to enjoy a glass of wine. The sense of normality that it gives me is pure joy.

I am amazed at the number of friends who are offering support and coming to visit. Everyone is rallying round with cards letters and phone calls. Even my cyber friends are in regular contact. Caroline and Jim, whom I've known since University, are driving down from Berkshire for the second time this month. I am bowled over at the effort they make just for one day. It is good to reminisce with them both about our shared experiences in Northern Ireland.

Ulster

I just don't have a clue how to revise properly and have worked myself up into frenzy before my exams. Being off sick for a month with hepatitis in my final year in the sixth form hasn't helped. As a consequence my A-level results are disappointing for me. I fail to get the B and two Cs needed to study languages at Sheffield so I am pooled back into the clearing scheme with my two Cs and a D. This puts me at the mercy of anonymous bureaucrats whose job it is to allocate surplus places.

They offer me a course at The New University of Ulster in Coleraine, Northern Ireland. I am to attend Magee College in Londonderry for the first two years, then a year out in Erlangen West Germany, followed by a final year in Coleraine. We discuss it and decide it is my only chance of a University education so I take it.

Mum is a little worried because of the troubles out there. She knows I have done my best and is as always totally supportive of my efforts.

The digs in Derry are grim. We aren't allowed any heat in the bedroom and there is frost on the inside of the windows. I am so cold that first winter that I have to get dressed in bed. A bath, which is designed to be a pleasant experience, is a weekly torture to be tolerated and completed as quickly as possible. By the time the hot tap fills the cold enamel tub the water is lukewarm; I miss my home comforts. Our landlady does not enjoy having 'students' and warns us she threw out her last tenants following a noisy party they held while she was away.

"I was so shocked," she relates dramatically. "I had to go next door for a Catholic cup of tea." She asks me if I am Catholic or Protestant. When I tell her I am Jewish, she looks at me strangely. She's never met one before and I suspect she is looking for a set of horns.

The German Conversation assistant joins the college in November. He brings his young son. All the local children ask him the same question: Catholic or Protestant?

"I'm a boy," is his innocent reply.

I meet up with Caroline and we spend a lot of time together, deciding that the Uni discos are not for us. We create our own entertainment with a small group of friends. Eventually we decide to rent a flat together, which we can then heat to our budget. It is in Great James Street on the edge of town. The rent is affordable and we take it. The wallpaper is peeling away and mildewed, but we attack it on a regular basis with a bottle of bleach. At least we have our own kitchen and bath. I use the word bath advisedly. It is not really a room, just a small cubicle with enough space for the tub. The sliding door keeps us warm, but if you push it too far it cascades down the stairs.

The first night we hear a strange noise, which sounds like someone screaming in pain. We pin it down eventually to the water pipes, which seem particularly vocal. The water from the taps sometimes emerges brown with a strange sludge-like quality. If it didn't taste so strongly of chlorine, Caroline and I are convinced there would be fish in it.

Ian Paisley holds a rally in Londonderry. One of our friends goes along out of curiosity. When he fails to clap at the right moment, men with black armbands come and throw him out, threatening to beat him up. Times are uncertain, the soldiers are nervous because children think it is good sport to throw stones at them. I meet a local Catholic guy who tells me his priest said it was okay to hurl petrol bombs at the British forces. He is disillusioned. I am horrified.

It is June 1970. There is supposed to be a rally in Bogside. Bernadette Devlin is due to address the crowds before handing herself over to the police following the collapse of her court appeal in December. Caroline and I hide away in the flat as we are told there could be riots. We are glad that we made that decision. Violence flares and we hear the distant sound of the petrol bombs and the angry populace. When I call Mum on the phone she is in panic. I reassure her we are safe.

My grant arrives and on an impulse I buy myself a guitar, determined to learn how to play. Once I tried at home on a steel string, which had been used as window dressing and was virtually unplayable; it made my fingers bleed. This model costs me twelve pounds and has nylon strings. I can't resist. One of our friends teaches me some basic chords and a beautiful classical piece called *Romanza*. It is way beyond my level of ability, but to the detriment of my first term's essay grades I finally master it.

Mum had never encouraged me musically since I couldn't easily hold a tune in my head. When I sang she told me to 'shut up' and when I practised recorder, I was banished to the bottom of the garden. "It'll be a nine day wonder," she pronounces, when I tell her about the purchase. I prove her wrong.

Of course with the guitar and the luxury of contact lenses, Caroline and I have to live on an extremely limited budget. Our diet is mostly porridge oats, vegetables, and small amounts of cheese or eggs. Luckily Caroline's Mum is a Cordon Bleu cook, so Caroline manages to produce amazing meals with limited ingredients and I learn a lot from her.

The lenses are worth it though they take some getting used to! We both sit in Professor J's class. He is puffing away on a pipe and the tobacco smoke irritates our eyes until they are red and streaming. We get used to the lenses eventually and dispense with our respective spectacles. What a joy.

The only time we are really affected by the Ulster troubles is in our final year at Coleraine. It is the twelfth of June 1973, after our written finals and Caroline and I are preparing to go home. I plan to go to the off licence to buy a bottle of Irish Whiskey to take back with me, but I wake with a banging headache following an over exuberant celebration party the previous evening. The decision not to go probably saves my life. We are disturbed by a massive explosion. The flat shakes. It seems a car bomb went off in Railway Road outside the bread shop, next to the Off Licence and the Travel Agent in town.

Caroline returns to the flat white and shaking. She describes the carnage: "I'd ridden my bike to the Travel Agent to buy my ticket home. I was paying for it, and she said 'Do you want to leave a deposit or pay?' and I said 'Oh a deposit,' and went to door. Then I thought 'This is stupid I'll pay for it now,' and walked back to the counter. At that moment there was an incredibly loud roaring noise – not like a roll of thunder, more like tanks at Sandhurst – and the glass window of the Travel Agency blew in. There was glass in my hair. I said 'What the hell was that?' and we all rushed to the back and stood in the yard. I said 'I've got to go home.' Eventually they let us go and they only way out was back through the shop. That was completely unreal, Lin." Caroline shivers, remembering. "I have snapshot memories. My memory is almost all yellow and white. Things seemed a different colour. It must have been dust. There was this guy that I thought I knew vaguely lying on a stretcher. You could only see his face, but he looked rather like roast pork. Sorry, but that's how he looked. He was completely black and all his skin was like crackling with marks all over it. I grabbed my bike and came back to the flat."

Caroline's story affects me deeply.

We read in the papers the next day that six civilians were killed. A five year-old child lost a leg. Ironically amongst the deceased is a couple who had come from Belfast for a day's shopping without threat of terrorism. They were killed instantly. Coleraine had come through the troubles unscathed thus far and this incident was the very first and last of its kind.

I go for my German oral exam the next day. I am to speak for about twenty minutes in German to demonstrate my fluency. The examiner asks me what I think is the most important thing to consider in the world today. I begin by saying that I find it hard to understand how academics can sit in ivory towers conducting these exams when children just a few hundred yards away are being blown to pieces.

I come away thinking my anger has got the better of me and I have failed; in fact I score well in the test. Thanks to the input of some superb lecturers, I have finally honed my skills in revision, and learn to have confidence in my ability. A more relaxed attitude to study helps me achieve an overall 2:1 BA Hons.

Though I am proud to be the first in my family with a University Degree, I run every time I see a parked car. I jump at the slightest noise. The effect lasts for weeks. I can't wait to leave Northern Ireland.

I have never been back, not even for graduation.

Diary – 17th September 2007

Levana rang me from Canada yesterday. "Grandma from England I have written you a letter. I love you so much the kisses are all on the back."

I have her other letters pinned up on the fridge door. She is only five years-old and hasn't quite grasped the separation of words, but what she writes is thrilling to read and brings tears to my eyes.

I love my Grandma England I think that you are nice
For my Grandma England I wish you are feeling better
I love my Grandma. She is a lovely Grandma.
I haven't got anybody who is as lovely as Grandma.

Levana is very special to me. I had gone to Canada to be there at her birth in 2002. I was due to fly back to the UK on the second of September for work. When Rachel hadn't gone into labour by the end of August she was in a flat panic. This was in part due to the fact that she thought she would never give birth, and the foetus would start shrinking back to nothing, and partly that she desperately wanted me to be there to support her.

Though I knew I should feel disappointed that I might miss the birth, I found it impossible to get stressed. Deep down I knew that it would turn out okay. Rachel was on pins. She saw every discomfort as a sign things were moving.

When the phone rang at two on the Friday morning she woke with a start. "The phone is ringing. It's ridiculous o'clock. I must be in labour."

In fact it was a friend who was ringing from abroad and who had forgotten about the time difference! By the time Rachel did go into labour early on Saturday morning it was just one day away from my having to leave Canada. By Saturday evening Rachel's pains were strong and rapid so I accompanied her to the hospital where I stayed with her all night.

FRMI
GRAMU
AREA.LAVEGRA

iLAVMiGRAMA
HSEEiZALAVLEG
RAMAiPOFHAVEN
AVLEASGRAMA

The following morning I saw Levana's head crowning. I hadn't witnessed the birth of either of my own two as they were both born by caesarean section. Watching my first granddaughter make her entry into the world was for me a unique miracle. I was even allowed to cut the cord before holding this precious baby in my arms, tears streaming down my face. A wave of emotion overwhelmed me.

Twenty minutes later I had to start my journey to the airport.

I cried most of the way home.

Birth

I was in a hospital room. All the doctors were dressed as tailors. They had tape measures and were fitting me for a larger tummy to suit my more advanced state of pregnancy. I didn't want a bigger tummy. The model they were offering was hideously distended and exceedingly uncomfortable. The nurses were laughing; I was in tears. It was at this point in my dream that my husband Paul nudged me from my uneasy slumbers with his anxious, "Are you all right?"

"Of course I am," I muttered, surfacing with relief in our own bed and making a swift check on the bulge under the bedclothes, which I gratefully acknowledged was the original.

"You were practising your breathing exercises."

I was wide-awake by then.

"I have to go to the bathroom," I said suddenly. Twenty minutes later I returned to the bedroom, shaking.

Fortunately Paul had the foresight to wake my Mum, who had arrived in Johannesburg a couple of days before. She took one look at me, half-in and half-out of bed, and unable to move.

"You're in labour my girl," she announced with a finality, which disintegrated all my doubts and left me feeling petrified and a little foolish.

I had been waiting for the low backache or tummy ache they had promised at antenatal clinic. This feeling of constipation as though

I was squeezing out a brick had not entered my plans.

"What shall I wear...? Ooooooh!" I yelped, alternately prancing up and down in front of the wardrobe and holding my spine as each spasm caught me.

"You're not going to a dinner party!" exclaimed Mum, exasperated with me already. "You're going to have a baby!"

And so the mad dash through the Johannesburg traffic began. At one-thirty am we finally arrived at the Park Lane clinic, where I was rushed straight to the labour ward, my contractions being less than two minutes apart. I was examined, purged and shaved. Initially they slowed the contractions with Pethidine, but later, as I was little more than two fingers dilated and becoming very exhausted they speeded them up with more drugs.

By eight am the gynaecologist had made his decision. "A caesarean section, I'm afraid, or a very difficult instrument delivery which might endanger you and the baby."

I remember the pain, and then the oblivion.

"Have I had a baby?" I asked the nurses when they came into my room.

"Oh yes," they said, taking my pulse.

"Well, is it a boy or a girl?"

"A girl, I think," said one, carefully smoothing an imaginary ruffle on my sheet. "I'll just go and check."

It was a well-held belief in South Africa in the mid-Seventies that babies should be trained into routines and not fed on demand. They held the babies together in the nursery. No mother was allowed to keep the baby with her. Any visitors would hear the familiar call, twice a day, "Time to see the babies!" and that was it. It struck me as strange, but I had to accept it.

It was difficult for me to bond with the tiny navy blue eyed infant they finally brought to my side. I couldn't really connect this baby with the pain and the subsequent surgery. One night the staff forgot to take the baby away. I spent the whole night just holding her and feeding her as and when she needed it. What a contrast. The following morning the flustered nurse came dashing into my room.

"Oh thank goodness. Thought you might have rolled over onto her." They really did believe that it was dangerous to leave new babies with their mothers!

A day or so later the staff nurse came in waving a bottle of water, telling me that baby might be thirsty. Within the hour another nurse came in and snatched it away.

"Breastfed babies don't need water!"

And so the farce would continue, day in day out. I didn't know whom to believe.

In contrast the birth of my son, in the UK two years later, was much less traumatic. I was warned that if I hadn't gone into spontaneous labour by the given date they would take me in for an elective caesarean. So it was that on the twenty-seventh of December 1978 I walked through the gates of the London Hospital Whitechapel and my son Daniel was born the following morning. I explained to the gynaecologist that I had felt detached and disorientated with the first birth, waking all alone and in unfamiliar surroundings. They assured me it would be different this time. They were right. I came round from the anaesthetic to the nurse's voice ricocheting round my head. "It's a boy, it's a boy, it's a boy."

"Can I see him?" I mumbled.

"'First we have to give you some more blood before we take you to the ward."

"That's ok," I reassured them from my drugged haze. "I have enough of my own, thank you."

I was soon holding my baby son in my arms for the first time. Daniel was allowed to be with me for the duration of my stay in hospital in a crib by my bed, and we bonded well. I demand fed him until he was nine months old with no problems. It was a wonderful experience.

Diary – 20th September 2007

Rachel rings me almost daily. She is struggling to come to terms with my illness and is concerned at the distance between us. The phone calls are a marvellous way for us to keep in contact.

Her calls are always entertaining. As we converse about how things are going her asides to Ziva are an eye-opener. "So how's it going, Mum? Hang on! Ziva… I don't think Batsheva likes being sat on like that. Sorry Mum, poor you – No, Ziva… don't grab her hand like that, you'll pull her fingers off. I'm trying to cook some – Ziva, you mustn't squeeze Batsheva's neck or she won't be able breathe…"

Clearly Batsheva will have to acquire some infant self-defence skills pretty quickly if she is to survive Ziva's form of 'Loving Terrorism' as described by Paul.

Being able to speak for an hour is a luxury. It is a far cry from the way things were for the four years I lived in South Africa with Paul.

Violation

Paul saw the move to South Africa in 1974 as an irresistible job opportunity and in some ways the lifestyle was fun. We enjoyed the outdoor 'breis' (barbeques) and the chance to swim most days in the summer months, thanks to the reliably good weather.

None of this was great compensation for me. I never really felt one hundred percent comfortable living in South Africa. The culture seemed alien. I felt very cut off from my family. We had to wait many months even to have a telephone installed, and the cost of calls was prohibitive. Nowadays I can ring Rachel on a cheap number and it costs a penny per minute. In 1976 it was about a pound a minute. We had to rely on letters, which might take up to two weeks to arrive. I felt extremely homesick and when Rachel was born it was exacerbated. I wanted family nearby. I was a young Mum in a foreign country with very little support.

Thirty-three years on and I think I have some understanding why you did it. You saw two vulnerable young women up on the ridge on that warm Johannesburg day, and you took your chance.

You probably acted out of desperation.

Many times I have asked myself why I wasn't frightened. I felt detached, as though I were watching a scene in a film.

My friend Pru had come to visit me, Paul, and our eight month-old baby Rachel in Johannesburg. Pru had been teaching in Zambia on a VSO scheme. Initially she suffered some culture shock. We had shops that actually sold things; we had roads; and luxury of luxuries – soap!

Pru spent those first few days marvelling at being back in civilisation with all its trimmings, such as hot water and electricity. We decided to go on a picnic on the ridge beyond the flats where we lived in Bedfordview. We took Rachel in her carrycot. Living so close meant that we didn't bother taking handbags or purses. We packed a bag of food, and for some musical recreation, a guitar. The morning air was still cool as we started our climb. Gradually the warm summer sun broke through the clouds in the mattress studded sky, highlighting the crystals of rock scattered on the grassy ridge as we picked our way over the scrubland and grasses to the summit.

In the distance we noticed a man dressed in a shabby dark blue jacket, and wearing a woollen hat, just looking at us. He was leaning on some sort of wooden stick, but we didn't think much of it. From the top of the ridge we had an aerial view of the whole town. We spread out our tartan blanket, put Rachel's carrycot under a tree for shade and began unpacking. We had just started to shell some of the fresh peas we'd brought for the picnic, when the man we had spotted earlier approached us. There was an acrid body smell as he came close. At first I thought he wanted to know the time, but then I noticed he was holding a knife.

His tone was clipped but demanding. "Give me your money!"

"We didn't bring any." I spoke without thinking. It was true of course, but clearly not very convincing to the assailant. He became very agitated. He went over to the carrycot wielding his knife menacingly.

"If you don't give me your money, I will hurt the baby"

"We are telling the truth. We didn't bring any money. You can search us if you want."

I wanted to distract him from the carrycot. We turned out our pockets. When he found not a cent on us he thought we were lying to him. He took my watch from my wrist and fortunately believed my half-hearted story that my wedding ring was stuck. With the terse command, "Don't move!" he grabbed our stuff and made off down the hill.

Pru and I waited until his figure was just a distant blur, then we packed up what was left and returned to the flats.

Still shocked, we went over the events as if we were establishing that it really had happened.

"I reckon we could have overpowered him, Lin, but I was worried about the baby. I'd have gone for him otherwise, knife or no knife. You do realise he could have chopped your finger off when you wouldn't give him your ring!"

"I know. I just didn't think. I couldn't bear the idea of him taking my wedding ring."

We were both miffed that he took our picnic; we had spent ages preparing it and had been looking forward to eating it.

Once Rachel had been safely handed over to our shocked neighbour, Pru and I went to report the incident to the Johannesburg police.

When we told our story we were taken aback by the policeman's response. "Ladies, I am telling you now, when we catch him his life won't be worth living!"

"But he didn't harm us," I explained. "He just threatened us and took all our stuff."

"He has molested two white women." The officer spat out the words in his clipped Afrikaans accent, his face rigid with disgust.

"But he had a knife. He could have killed us! He had nothing to loose," we protested.

"It makes no difference. Just wait until we catch him. Now, can you give me a thorough description?"

It was at that point my allegiances changed. My anger turned to pity, and suddenly I had a deep sense of injustice.

At the ID parade I was dreading seeing your face. I was shaking in case I saw you there and had to pick you out. I felt tremendous relief when I didn't recognise you in any of the men in the line; they all wore the woolly cap and the shabby clothes.

At that moment I realised the violation hadn't been against us, two affluent white women up at Gilooly's.

It was against you.

Diary – 23rd September 2007

My appetite is returning slowly. I can eat most things now without side effects, but I still have to be careful about quantity. Though I am picky about food, having had such horrendous experiences at Primary School, I don't consider myself to be as fussy as Dad was.

I think back to those days at Ardwell Avenue and how difficult it was for my poor Mum to please his palate. I can only commend her tolerance of his idiosyncrasies. She had a lot to put up with!

Life at Ardwell Avenue

I know it drove Mum to despair that her innovative experiments in cookery were met with such resistance. Dad wanted steak, or egg and chips, roast beef and Yorkshire pudding, sausage and mash, liver and onions, but balked at anything slightly foreign sounding. Offered Ratatouille or Quiche he would shrug and express his distain with his favourite comment: "I'm not enamoured," smothering the bulk of Mum's culinary creations with HP sauce. It broke her inventive spirit, so our diet remained pretty much unchanged through the decades. The nearest she came to succeeding with foreign fare was spaghetti Bolognese, where Mum substituted ketchup for brown sauce.

At heart Mum was a great traditional roast dinner cook. She loved her meat, and would prefer a second helping of beef or lamb to a dessert. Throughout my childhood the house would fill with the smells of Sunday Roast as *Family Favourites* and *Round the Horn* played in the back ground on the BBC Home Service. Dad was picky about meat. A bad experience in the army saw the corpse of a hapless headless bird he was plucking jump from his hands and scoot off into the distance. It put him off chicken for life.

Mum's roast beef was crispy on the outside, tender in the middle. Unfortunately the oven, which had served her well since 1969, had deteriorated in performance by the Eighties. Mum simply didn't notice. It was a gas oven, with a separate hob. I first realised when I brought a cake mix over to bake for Dan's birthday. It was a tried and tested recipe, but came out like a pancake. Then the Sunday roasts took longer and longer to cook.

"Mum," I explained gently. "This oven really isn't cooking things well any more. I think there is a problem with the gas pressure."

Mum remained adamant. "I've had this oven for twenty years. It's fine." It clearly wasn't.

Dad wouldn't contemplate rare meat. It had to be done to death before he would eat it. One Sunday we prepared the lunch. The familiar smell of boiling cabbage permeated the living room. Mum brought the beef triumphantly to the table. I helped with the vegetables. We raised our knives and forks expectantly as carving began… then we realised; the joint was scarcely warm and decidedly raw on the inside. Rare doesn't even come close.

Mum and Dad

"How long did you give it, Frances?" Dad queried, thinking she had maybe made some mathematical error. Mum was deeply affronted.

"I put it in at eleven. It should be done by now." It was one-thirty.

Mum had to finally concede there was a problem when some of the outer slices of beef did not become remotely edible until three-fifteen, heralding the end of our oven's useful life.

By my next visit Mum and Dad proudly showed off their newest acquisition. It was a microwave that could also bake. I noticed that the broken oven was still there taking up considerable space in the already cramped kitchen.

"Why don't you have this taken away?" I tentatively suggested.

Mum opened the oven door proudly. There inside she had neatly stacked all her Pyrex dishes and baking trays.

"See I told you I could find a use for it."

The appliance had simply become another 'YNK' – Mum's unique form of recycling: You Never Know (when you might need it). Further persuasion was pointless.

Dad's drawer was neat and tidy. Mum had piles of paper around the place. She wrote all her memos and reminders on scraps, which were stock-piled round the room. My one attempt to get her organized with a diary simply ended up with a relocation of all the paper inside the diary. She didn't have the heart to use up the pages!

One day I went round to find her wiping the work surfaces with a J-cloth that was sadly lacking in cloth. I held it up to the light.

"Mum, what an earth is this?" It had been through the washing machine so many times that the holes were loosely strung together with shreds of material, like netting. Mum looked a bit meek. "I didn't realise. It is a bit threadbare!"

"A bit threadbare! It's thin air with a blue and white border! Come on, treat yourself to a new one!"

Mum bent down and took a pack of fifty from the cupboard. Must have been the 'waste not want not' war years that influenced her.

Mum wore a mask of confidence. It was the only face she wanted to show to the wide world. With me she would take it off, and confess with what little regard she held herself. When I went to University she was afraid that I would not want my friends to meet her because she was 'working class'. It was a faulty cognition that took me a lot of persuasion to change. This mask helped her cope with her low self esteem.

Mum was also the rescuer in her 'Knight in Shining Armour' mask. She would help anyone who needed it. She put herself out a lot for others and this mask helped her feel good about herself. If she was helping others then she felt validated. She needed to do this very frequently or she didn't feel worthy despite being told lots of times by those who liked, admired or loved her just how great she was. This mask was so necessary to her and yet it was destructive. She always put others first so there was no time for her own needs.

When Gerald was first married in the Seventies ,Mum was amazing to her new daughter- in- law and nothing was too much trouble for her. She was badly hurt when Gerald's marriage broke up. She had given so much. I am not sure she ever really recovered from the rejection she experienced. I noticed how cold she was towards Teresa, Gerald's second wife. It was as if she was trying to protect herself from further damage. We talked it through.

"Mum, do you realise that you are sometimes quite cool and unfriendly towards Teresa?"

"Well, once bitten twice shy. I just don't want to make the same mistake twice. You know what happened between me and Carol."

"I understand you are still hurt, but none of this is Teresa's fault. At least give her a chance."

Mum's manner with Teresa was noticeably warmer after that.

Mum was the 'tough nut' who wouldn't be cracked. This mask was for folk she didn't get on with, or authority that let her down. She stood for no nonsense. By wearing this mask she could protect the tender centre inside herself. Mum was like an egg. The tough outer shell just covered a soft interior.

Dad was short, about five feet five inches, good looking, stocky and unbelievably hairy. My earliest memories see him bare-chested and shaving in front of the mirror. I would flee from his chest hairs, which terrified me, and had me hiding under the table. Sitting on his lap I would spend chunks of time trying to tug on his beard hairs. He convinced me that they were actually all attached and if I pulled correctly I could unravel them in one long coil. Dad played the game with gusto, flinching each time I attempted to tweak a hair. Despite this he found it difficult to be demonstrative with us kids; probably because his own mother showed little in the way of outward signs of love. When I cried, which I often did in those days, he quickly lost patience and I acquired the nickname of 'Waterworks'. It was a label that stuck with me throughout my childhood. I loathed it.

Mum was the sensible one and was quick to rein Dad in when he became irate or obstinate. One evening they had invited his sister over for dinner. Around nine-thirty, whilst Mum and Aunty Hannah were deep in conversation, Dad rose quietly from the chair and went upstairs.

Aunty Hannah was proudly telling us about her son, "He nearly got a place at Oxford, but they were full!" when Dad made his re-entry into the lounge in his pyjamas, dressing gown and slippers. Mum shrivelled with embarrassment, whilst Dad remained unfazed. Hannah looked slightly taken aback, but only when Dad began pointedly yawning and looking at his watch, did she eventually take the hint and leave. Mum was beside herself.

"Jimmy you can't do that. It's rude."

"I was tired. I wanted to go to bed."

I don't know what else Mum said to him later that night but he didn't repeat the performance.

Dad was pretty pedantic in most things. A creature of habit he would scour the *Daily Mirror*, potter about, 'fix things' that did or didn't need fixing. When Rachel and Daniel were young he would give them a tour of the garage and they would come away clutching some dangerous 'toy' that might have shards of exposed metal, leaking batteries and wood splinters. The kids loved it. He even had nine year-old Daniel wielding a hammer to knock in some fence posts.

And Dad was of course a bit of an embarrassment. Gregarious by nature he would spontaneously speak to strangers who seemed to warm to him. On a family trip to Cologne in the late Eighties, he managed to get lost in a department store. He spoke no German, but was determined to look at a Soda Stream, which was all the rage at the time. Dad started gesturing what he thought was the Soda Stream mechanism, pumping his arm up and down in determined fashion. They understandably misunderstood his needs and directed him to the toilet. He pressed G for what he thought was 'ground floor' and ended up in the Garage Car Park. He was found eventually by ten year-old Daniel and twelve year-old Rachel.

Towards the end of the Eighties, I volunteered to go over for a weekend to help paint the lounge and cover over the nicotine stains. Dad took Rachel and Daniel to a local restaurant for lunch and Mum and I continued decorating.

"Mum," they protested on their return. "He started talking to the waitress and we disowned him. We pretended he was some geezer escaped from an old folks home. Don't ever do that to us again..."

After Mum died Dad's behaviour changed. Free of her gentle restraint he became idiosyncratic in his behaviours. After Mum's funeral we had a house full of relatives. Dad became agitated when he found a hand towel in the downstairs toilet covered in brown stains.

He held up the towel in disbelief. He was red in the face shocked and angry.

"That's it...I'm locking the toilets."

"Dad, you can't do that… it's only Mum's hair dye."

He took some convincing.

Mum had always made a point of ringing me on my birthday. I was well into adulthood but looked forward to her call: "Hello, Birthday Girl". I felt loved and special. She never forgot. Things were so different with Dad. He would present me with my card about three months before my birthday in case he forgot.

"Here," he'd say, handing me a card in an envelope that had seen better days "Look after this. Buy yourself a present and I'll give you the money."

Of course I said, "Thanks Dad" and I tried to mean it, but it was never easy. My birthday would come and go, unmarked by even a phone call. Sometimes I found an old yellowed Christmas card in the envelope. Dad hadn't bothered to check. I would hear Mum's voice in my head: "Jimmy, you can't do that," but he did, year on year.

Of course I was fond of Dad, but I didn't really look forward to visiting. I would walk up to the front door to be greeted by a sign on the wall in Dad's wobbly print smudged with ink and stuck inside a torn bit of polythene: NO CALLERS!

"That's a bit extreme," I commented as he opened the door.

"I'm fed up with the Jehovah's witnesses and people selling stuff."

"Fair enough, but what about your relatives… like me?"

Dad just shrugged and the sign stayed. Conversation was heavy going. He liked to talk about his rotary washing line. He'd persuaded me to purchase one of the same make several years before. So instead of the usual, "Hello how are you?" I would often hear "So how's the washing line? You know you'll never buy a better one. It'll last you a lifetime."

"Then why ask?" I often wondered, but out of deference I kept the comment to myself. When that topic had been thrashed to death he might start on his 'Henry', a small vacuum cleaner with two eyes, a nose and (to Dad) a personality.

“Quality that is! Picks up the bits a treat. You should get one. It’ll never let you down. You know they use them in all the hotels now.”

I knew of course. Dad had told me on my last six visits.

First time Dad stayed with Chris and me on the Isle of Wight, I took him on a tour of the house. From the back bedroom we have a stunning view of the sea. Dad came upstairs and looked out the window. Ignoring the beautiful view across the Solent his gaze went straight down into the garden. “What a washing line! That’ll last you a lifetime that will!”

Diary – 27th September 2007

It is six am. I don't have to be up but pre-dawn my brain switched itself on without warning. The first of my two Southampton scans is tomorrow. It is a special CT PET scan which involves my being injected with radioactive glucose. I am to starve for six hours prior to the scan and have to rest all day today. This is a contrast with my gradual ability to increase my activities over the past couple of weeks now that the pain has receded. I feel frustrated that I am once more housebound, that I have to undergo further invasive treatment. Because of the contaminant in my system I won't be allowed near pregnant women or babies, but what effect will this have on me?

Outside autumn is making its presence felt. There is a distinct chill in the northerly wind. The swimming season is coming to an end soon. Will I be able to take it up again next spring? I struggle to accept the dramatic changes to my lifestyle.

My Head of Department called in on Tuesday evening. She is being incredibly supportive. It is a wrench to leave all my work colleagues and to cut myself off from what is happening there, but I know I have to. I have been teaching in schools since 1974.

Loughton County High

My first teaching post, early Seventies, is in a tough north west London comprehensive. I am in my probationary year, a novice. My Head of Department contracts malaria in the summer holiday and is on long term sick. I have no guidance and a class of thirty -three unruly Second Years who do not want to learn a foreign language.

Friday afternoon and this unteachable class come in quietly, take their seats, sit in silence and look up expectantly. It is wholly unnerving. A sea of faces and they are all focused on me. Then the cold realisation hits me. The Deputy Head has followed them in and all I have prepared is a worksheet. I am completely wrong-footed. In desperation I demonstrate the first few sentences calling volunteers to the board to try out the answers. We work through all the questions orally before I ask them to fill in the sheet for themselves. They even show enthusiasm, keen to demonstrate what they know. Instead of shouting out randomly, they put their hands up. Bliss. By today's standards the lesson would probably be slated, but the Deputy Head is clearly impressed. He tells me afterwards

"You have the makings of an excellent teacher. You obviously prepare your material well."

I mutter something about the lesson only working because he had been there, but he is utterly dismissive of my plea for more support.

"Don't worry about discipline," he tells me. "Last year we had a teacher smaller than you. The kids were terrified of her."

That is the sum total of his advice in the three years I teach at the school. Happy days.

I stay two years, leaving eventually when I am pregnant with my first child. Paul's job takes us to South Africa in 1976. We are loathe to bring up children under the harsh Apartheid system, and opt to return to the UK in 1978. In 1981 when Rachel is about to start school I manage to find a job in a large Dagenham comprehensive. The Deputy Head is a bully. It is a hot and sultry Friday afternoon. I arrive at the classroom on the other side of the large rambling building to teach a group of difficult Third Years. To my horror I discover the room is locked and we have to wait ages for the key; none of this helps their bouncy behaviour.

We are just entering the class when the Deputy Head marches sternly through the door and announces in front of all the pupils, "This is an unacceptably noisy group."

I am furious, and refuse to be intimidated.

"Excuse me," I counter. "We have all been waiting for the last twenty minutes in the corridor because the room was locked. We have only just this minute got in here."

Thereafter the Deputy Head takes to smiling at me, but I feel that I am not happy working for such an unprofessional colleague, so I look around for a new position. I want something more local to where we live. I go for a job in Loughton, a few blocks from the house and to my delight I get it. The post is Head of German in a small Girls' Comprehensive. It suits me well. I am pleased to say goodbye to large schools in rough areas. My Fifth Year non-examination class are challenging, but working in Willesden and Dagenham respectively, I have honed a few classroom management skills to help me cope.

My very first lesson with them turns out to be trial by fire. I guess there will be trouble when Coral nonchalantly peels a tangerine in front of me. When I give her my 'stern' look she shrugs.

"Don't worry miss. I'm not going to eat it. It's for the RE lesson."

I have just finished my eloquent delivery when Katy gets up and strolls across the room, takes a brush from Coral's bag and begins grooming her hair.

"I don't remember giving you permission to leave your seat," I remonstrate calmly.

She responds with a cheeky "You would have said no."

I am proud of my quick repartee:"And how long have you been practising mind-reading?"

First round to me. I am beginning to feel I have the upper hand with the group, when, from the corner of my eye I notice an object fly across the room. To my dismay I see that it is a sanitary towel. I realise with sickening dread that there is an unmistakeable red smear on it.

Not wanting to show my shock, I turn to face the board. From the safety of my hiding place I say boldly and clearly, "Would someone put that disgusting object in the bin?"

"It's ok, Miss." (Coral again). "It's only nail polish."

I spend the remaining half an hour trying desperately not to shake. My calm responses eventually win them over and we have a reasonably smooth year until they leave.

During my second term, a letter to parents is distributed, warning about an outbreak of head lice in a second year class. I have to cover 2e Drama but am horrified to discover it is to be a practical session. I have to observe the class performing sketches set in, of all places, a hairdressing salon!

As the students enthusiastically brandish their brushes and combs, I cower as far from the action as I dare, practising unobtrusive ways to scratch my head. Luckily I am spared an infestation.

At the end of term I take my tutor group on a sponsored walk. Eleven year-old Devina eagerly tells us of her weekend encounter with a flasher. She is not bothered by the lack of counselling for post-traumatic stress disorder. She wants to show us exactly where it happened. It takes a lot of persuasion to move her on. I am relieved when we return to school without incident only to discover one group is an hour late. The Geography teacher got lost following the map.

Many years later I meet an ex-Special Educational Needs student of mine, now in Year Eleven who has also moved schools. I taught her when she was Year Seven. Whatever instruction I gave to the class, she always managed to misinterpret.

"Hello Miss," she calls out cheerfully. "I remember everything you ever taught me!"

I seriously doubt that, but it leaves me smiling.

I spend a very happy five years at Loughton until the Local Education Authority go through a massive shake up of education and amalgamation of small schools. I am loath to teach in a large comprehensive again so we decide to move to a different area rather than send our own children to such an establishment.

Diary – 2nd October 2007

The first scan is over. It was in a mobile lorry outside the BUPA hospital in Southampton.

The man who administers the radioactive isotope is friendly and informs me that each injection costs £400, which is why he inserts a canula; he can't afford to take a risk that the vein might collapse. He tells me that he will leave the glucose to go round my body for about twenty-five minutes, then he will return. I am surprised when the sliding door opens after only a couple of minutes. He looks at me oddly.

"Can I ask you a personal question?" His tone is tentative and I wonder what on earth he means. "They have ringed male…"

The words mean nothing to me and I ask for an explanation. He shows me the paperwork. Where it says MALE/ FEMALE I am down as the former!

I assure him that I am definitely female, and can't help chuckling.

"I have to ask," he says. "We sometimes have transvestites."

I am wearing loose comfortable trousers, dingly-dangly earrings, and my name is Linda… should I be worried?

He is clearly relieved that I am not offended. So much so that when he returns after the prerequisite half hour he says, "Ready when you are, sir!"

I have received a letter from an ex-colleague, Linda. She always described herself as 'mad as a hatter', but she has excelled herself this time. She has sent me some Holy Water from St Winifred's Well, which apparently cured her dog of liver problems. She knows I am Jewish, but writes: "Holy water is for everyone… Suggest you drink a little, put some on your tummy where your liver is and put some on your forehead for it can relieve stress of the mind by doing that and so help the body. As we live in a free country none of this is compulsory though."

I will of course drink the Holy Water and rub it in as suggested. I will try anything. I doubt her dog was a Catholic but it worked for him…

I can hear Linda's voice in my head and am taken back to those crazy times at the High School when we were doing the German orals together.

Life with Linda

I have come from a state comprehensive in Loughton to a Girls' Public Day School Trust. It is 1987, and the GCSE exams are to go ahead this year for the first time, replacing GCE and CSE. I hadn't sought work in the private sector, but was head-hunted by a previous Head of Languages. As Paul and I wanted to move to the Kent area because of reorganisation, I went for the post.

The Head of German, Linda, is highly eccentric and absolutely lovely. You couldn't wish to meet a warmer, friendlier person. She still dresses in a 1950s style and is proud of it. Her hair is mid-length and beginning to grey. Her voice is strident and she likes to be noticed. When the phone rings in the staff room she picks it up with a confident, " Battersea Home for the Bewildered!" It doesn't bother her that the Headteacher is sometimes on the line. She just adds a nonchalant: "Oh Good Morning, Mrs H."

In Linda's classroom she is often seen standing on a table to demonstrate a point of German grammar, much to the amusement of her captive audience. At interview she spoke to me in impeccable German. Afterwards she revealed, "Your German was two hundred percent better than the other candidate!"

Soon after I start my job Linda confides in me.

"I am so glad you are here. I haven't a clue about the GCSE and I am going to need your advice and expertise. We have to conduct, assess and tape all the oral exams ourselves." She lowers her voice "Between you and me, I have never managed to work out how to use a cassette recorder."

I am working for a self-confessed Luddite. I can see there will be challenging times ahead.

Linda and I will run the exams together. Linda will examine her students and I will assess, then we will swap roles. The two of us are more nervous than the candidates. For each individual I have to double check that the tape is set to record and I need to remember to release the pause button. We also have to make sure that the role play cards are given randomly to each girl, and that they are returned to us at the end. We have to time the interviews without making it obvious to the examinees. Nerve-wracking. We have to ask each student a finite number of questions spread over several topics, followed by an interactive role play where the card shows the scenario (café, garage, town centre, etc) and what they have to communicate.

It starts off well enough, but our star pupil whose German is exceptional upsets the smooth rhythm. I begin by asking her name and where she lives. She announces her answers fluently and in a well-rehearsed staccato voice. She rattles off her address in perfect German, but just as I am about to ask the next question about hobbies, she suddenly cuts me short and declares, "POSTLEITZAHL," proceeding to add the post code all the numbers and letters being spot on perfect.

I look at Linda, who has been allocating marks, and I can see that her shoulders are shaking. I have to swallow my own laughter for the remainder of the examination. I can only do this by concentrating intently on my candidate and not allowing my eyes to stray to the back of the room where Linda is continuing to struggle with her suppressed mirth. When the candidate leaves we both burst into hysterics.

After that, it seems there is one crazy incident after another. I put out my hand to take the role-play cards from one girl, who misunderstands the gesture, leaves the cards on the table and vigorously shakes my hand for several minutes. Between candidates Linda and I laugh uncontrollably. It relaxes my nerves and somehow we make it through the day without visible hitch.

Linda is unendingly grateful. I had not envisaged my first batch of self-conducted oral exams to be quite like that!

I enjoy the classroom work. The GCSE course emphasises different skills from the old style GCE, and my first batch of results is excellent, enabling some girls to perform far better than they expected. I receive a note from one of my students, Amelia: *I'd like to thank you for the amazing recovery you have given to my German during the past year. I had given up.*

Though I am happy working with the students, the five years I spend at the school are not happy. The senior staff have unreasonable expectations of extra curricular commitments unrelated to pupil progress. One day the Deputy Head marches towards me clutching her desk diary: "Since you didn't attend the governor's meeting last night, I will put you down for helping at the Careers Evening tomorrow."

I am determined not to be bulldozed and respond assertively. "If you do not feel that I am doing my job properly, please tell me. Otherwise I will decide which meetings I do or don't attend."

My answer falls on stony ground. I have scuppered my chances of promotion, but I don't mind.

The Deputy Head leaves me alone thereafter, but I notice how insidiously she manages to perpetuate an ethos of bullying with some staff. She tries to involve me with a colleague. "I notice that Carol was shouting at you in the staff room this morning. I find that behaviour totally unacceptable."

I am speechless, but later that evening I realise what she is alluding to. I decide to confront her the following day. "I want to clear up a misunderstanding about yesterday. Carol was just sounding off generally. Her comments were not directed at me."

I sense that the Deputy Head is unhappy with my attempt to protect Carol. Carol feels she is a victim and that she has no option other than to leave her job.

I am grateful to my Mum for teaching me to stand up for myself.

It upsets me to see good colleagues hounded out of the workplace. I can cope with the likes of the Deputy Head and other senior staff who take a similar stance. What finally drives me to leave is the Headteacher's attitude. I feel that my teaching expertise is undervalued. I give my all to the job, as I have done since I started teaching. When I went through the painful divorce process, I did not ask for a single day's leave of absence. When we move house on a Thursday I ask for the additional Friday to get the place straight. The Head refuses my request and insists that I also attend the Celebration Day on the Saturday. I am devastated. To me this is a slap in the face.

I deliberately miss the Saturday commitment, and I make the decision to return to the state sector where my skills will be recognised and appreciated. I need a good reference so I say nothing about my grievances. I accept a job in a West Kent comprehensive.

After two years there when my Mum dies, the Deputy tells me to take as much time as I need. What a contrast.

Diary – 3rd October 2007

Today we go to Southampton for the MRI scan.

I find out that a woman on one of my favourite website forums (who has battled with cancer for the last five years) finally lost her fight for life. She died. It leaves me feeling scared stiff.

We plan a nice bit of 'retail therapy' in West Key Southampton in the morning and then go on to the hospital. The receptionist is particularly helpful and tells us that there is guest accommodation for Chris on site when I have the liver operation. One of the volunteers in the MRI reception latches onto Chris, follows us into the waiting room, and begins describing the catalogue of ailments that have befallen her over the last few years. She makes eye contact with the ceiling, always a bad sign, and her bombardment is unrelenting. I can see the glazed expression on Chris' face.

When I go to the interview room prior to the scan he opts to come with me to escape her clutches. As we leave the room she goes off to seek out her next victim. It must be sad to be so lonely.

The scan is long and drawn out. It takes an hour. I have to have two injections of dye, but the radiologist fails to insert a canula in my right arm. She then tries my right hand. Neither attempt is successful. The chief radiologist appears out of nowhere and digs around in my left arm, eventually succeeding in penetrating a vein in my wrist. At this point I can't stop the tears. I have had so many needles; this is just three too many. I have to hold my breath many times for up to twenty-five seconds on the out breath. It isn't easy, especially when I just want to cry my eyes out and go home. I am relieved when they finally release me.

When my friends telephone or visit, some just aren't sure what to say. I sense their discomfort. I'm not sure what to say either.

Over twenty years go, when Mum rang me and told me what happened to Gerald, I was in total panic. What would I say to him?

I can remember people avoiding me when my parents died.

Perhaps our society does not equip us to cope with illness, disability or death.

Gerald's Leg

I peered through the smeared glass surprised at the pallid face that stared back at me as the tube rattled into the tunnel. Blackfriars. I glanced briefly towards the doors, hoping for some relief from the oppressive heat, but the blast of hot smutty air merely added to my discomfort. Each of the eight station stops was bringing me closer to the dreaded moment.

I noticed the man opposite, thirty-ish, dark, enigmatic, the shadow of a beard encasing his sallow face. His angular features reminded me of Gerald. As our eyes met fleetingly, I felt an uncontrolled surge of resentment and quickly turned back to the privacy of the window. He was probably off to work, just being ordinary.

I thought of Gerald lying in his hospital bed coping with the pain and loss. He'd gone to the doctors complaining of pains in his leg. The GP diagnosed cramp and gave him some tablets. Two weeks later and he was in agony. It turned out to be a deep vein thrombosis. At that time laser treatment was not available. To save his life they had to amputate just below the knee. Mum was devastated. She felt terrible, because she had named Gerald after Woolf, Dad's brother. He'd lost his leg and then his life, in World War II, from a leg injury that had turned gangrenous. She felt that she was somehow responsible.

I could picture myself walking into the ward at the Royal London Hospital, smelling the antiseptic, but try as I might the rest was a blur. A shared childhood, twenty-eight years of closeness, but he'd gone into the hospital whole, and was now minus one leg. What on earth would I say to him?

As the train approached Whitechapel I picked myself up and resolutely battled my way towards the doors. One way or another I had to do this.

When I walked into the ward my heart was pounding, my mouth dry, my limbs shaking. Then a strange transformation occurred. In the bed I didn't see the amputee I was expecting. I saw my brother Gerald lying there. He looked thin and pale but he was my brother, just as he'd always been and I talked to him, just as I always had. Relief washed over me as I sank into the chair by his bed.

Diary – 4th October 2007

Today I see the cancer specialist, Dr B. He asks me if I have had the scans. I wonder why he doesn't already know, and it hardly fills me with confidence.

He disappears for several minutes to make some phone calls. When he returns he shares the findings with us both. The detailed scans have highlighted five liver tumours. They will give me twelve weeks of treatment before taking more scans. If the tumours have shrunk then they will operate before giving me another three-month course of chemotherapy.

Dr B tells me that he will book me a chemo appointment in two weeks. He introduces me to the research nurse who is co-ordinating the trial. I have a week to decide if I want to go ahead. Chris tries to persuade me to volunteer. I am unsure whether to subject my body to even more chemicals. We take away the leaflets to read.

We go and look at the Chemotherapy Suite. It is in a remote part of the hospital, on an upper level, past long ceiling pipes and strange locked cupboards. We go up in a lift that is more suited to transit than people. The suite itself appears out of place in such strange surroundings, but the waiting room is welcoming. The nurse in charge takes us round. Patients are sitting in comfy recliners. I am relieved to see they are not screaming in agony and that they look peaceful. The charge nurse wants to do an initial assessment a few days prior to the commencement of the first session.

Now that treatment is about to start I am getting cold feet. I am loath to be a guinea pig for new treatment, because it involves weekly drips and lots more medical interventions. I want to bottle out.

I wake at 3am when I am at my most vulnerable, and the realisation hits me like a sledgehammer. The treatment is going to last twice as long as I had expected. I have to face a major operation and then more of the same.

When I had Rubella at aged ten, I was in tears: "But, Mummy, I don't want spots!"

I feel the same about these five tumours.

The interventions may not work. If there were an injection that I could have right now that would take me away from all this I would opt for it.

I talk it through with Chris at dawn. He is understanding, but when I go for a morning swim he is already speculating on what he will say to the police when I don't return. "Oh, she goes for a swim most days when the tide is right. I would have gone with her but I wanted a lie-in. She must have been swept away." It had crossed his mind that I might deliberately swim out and keep going.

We can laugh about it now, but my feelings of hopelessness swamp me like a dark blanket and I struggle to shake them off. I think I need some time to come to terms with all these changes.

A change in direction

It takes an encounter with a particularly obstreperous student to guide me towards a new career path.

I've dealt with huge numbers of students in more than twenty years of mainstream teaching, but it is Paul who leaves the most indelible imprint. He wasn't that striking; a bit conspicuous because of his height, with a voice you couldn't ignore. But he was special. I met him at a crucial time – and it was an encounter that changed my life.

I inherited Paul's Year Ten class when I joined the West Kent comprehensive in 1992. I was their eighth Modern Languages teacher that academic year. They had spent the previous term honing their skills in Origami and the art of hurling paper aeroplanes. My seven predecessors had succeeded in delivering about ten words of German to them, nine of which they had forgotten. I wasn't surprised that they lacked motivation and confidence. They were a tough class, but they did refer to me as their first 'proper' teacher. I took it as a compliment.

My personal life was a mess; a recent divorce had left me bereft and miserable. I was upset that my children were experiencing the pain of separation from their father, who had left us all for a younger woman.

Autumn 1993 had been a stressful term for me. I was trying to organise an exchange trip to Germany for my students, but also having to come to terms with the fact that my mother was in a hospice dying of cancer. The days seemed to pass in pointless blur of commuting, working, visiting the hospice, cooking and cleaning. I faced an emotional winter far more daunting than the seasonal one.

Paul was our classroom tsunami. When he spoke it was louder than everyone else. He would suddenly shout across the room magnetising the group to respond at similar volume. He craved attention; any sort. I rarely shouted, but on this particular October day, I was on a shorter fuse than usual. I lost my cool with Paul. The class was taken aback when I sent him to work in the open area next to the Deputy Head's office.

A few minutes later the Deputy entered the classroom. The Year Tens were working in stunned silence following my outburst. At first I thought she wanted to talk to me about Paul – then I saw her expression.

My brother was on the telephone. My mother had fallen into a coma.

I remember stepping out of the office visibly in tears. I might have expected resentment on Paul's face as he sat in isolation. Instead he showed me compassion, which was reflected in his words. "Are you alright Miss?"

I told Paul that my Mum was dying.

Thereafter my relationship with Paul changed. He never disrupted my lessons again. Paul, who rarely volunteered an answer, put up his hand seven times when the Ofsted inspector visited. Paul started hanging back after class chatting to me about what was going on in his life. He was mixing with the wrong crowd and was in trouble with the police.

Paul was terrified of a court conviction. From underneath the tough exterior, I gradually uncovered the frightened little boy. His words at the end of 1993 encapsulated our shared troubles: "It's been a lousy year one way or another, hasn't it, Miss?"

I have a lot to thank you for, Paul. In that unguarded October moment you saw my sadness and vulnerability. In return you allowed me a glimpse into your life. Your trust in me gave me the inspiration and courage to make a change of direction. I became a counsellor working with students who have Emotional and Behavioural Difficulties. Many of them have confided in me over the years. I won't forget you, Paul, because you were the first.

Mum dying hits me hard. I survived divorce only with her unerring support throughout, and now I feel alone and bereft. There is no one who loves me quite like she did; who cares about my successes, who has an interest in what I am doing and how things are going. So I gradually come to terms with that harsh reality and it proves to be a painful path to tread. Mum was proud I had realised my ambition to become a teacher.

"It's a good profession. You will always find a job. Stick with it."

While she was alive I believed those statements to be the truth. Mum's death at age sixty-seven allows me to confront my own mortality. It helps me realise that I am unhappy in my job and sometimes dread the days with difficult classes. Without her cautionary warnings I am freed to make a life changing career decision.

Meeting Paul is the trigger. I am given some bereavement counselling through my local LEA and during the final few sessions I begin to be attracted to the idea of becoming a counsellor. I find out everything I can about it and embark initially on an evening class Certificate in Counselling to see if it is the right direction for me.

Six months later, clutching my certificate, I start looking for a suitable diploma course. I resign my full-time job teaching at the Kent comprehensive with no job to go to. I trust I can find something part time to see me through the two-year course. Rachel and Daniel support me, and accept that money will be a little tight for a while.

In June of the same year, a part-time job comes up at a Catholic school in Bexley. I take the job for three days a week. It leaves me the time to do the diploma. In the second year of the course the school beg me to take on another day. Reluctantly I agree. It improves our finances but life is difficult. I teach all day, then go on to the GP surgery for my placement after school, sometimes returning home at nine or ten pm. I then have to record the detailed notes for each counselling session. It is tough going. On a Saturday morning I travel to Penge for a second placement to ensure I have the requisite one hundred counselling hours. It turns out to be an exhausting year but knowing there is an end in sight helps me through.

In the January I manage to swap jobs and go to work for the Kent County Council Behaviour support service, which gives me more opportunities to practise my newly acquired counselling skills. I am deployed into various schools to work with students one-to-one, and to contribute to staff training with a team of people.

My first breakthrough comes with Chrissie. She is in Year Seven, referred for severe emotional and behavioural problems in class. Sometimes she refuses to speak at all and will hide under the desk or play with her hair, making noises like a three year-old. We do a lot of story work and pictures together, but after many weeks we make little progress. She never misses a session with me, so I stick with it. Eventually she discloses physical abuse from her mother. She shows me the bruises, and with her permission we go through the teacher in charge of Child Protection to call in Social Services. Chrissie is taken into temporary foster care while the problems at home are sorted out.

I work with Sara for several months. She is a Year Ten girl with a history of bullying younger children. In class she exhibits loud attention-seeking behaviours. When she was referred she was on the verge of permanent exclusion and had had a string of temporary exclusions behind her. We work on self-esteem building exercises and assertiveness skills. Sara begins to learn how to speak in a way that ensures she is listened to. Over time as her self-awareness and self-esteem increase she is able to develop empathy. I tell her about one of her peers, Louise, who has come to me in tears because of Sara's friend who has been throwing rubbers at her in class and making fun of her. I speak to Sara about it.

"I am upset to see someone so unhappy. Do you think there is anything you could do to help?"

Sara, who had been systematically bullying other children since she was in Year Seven, speaks to Louise: "It's ok. She don't mean nothing by it. Don't worry about it."

In the following lessons, Sara persuades her friend to leave Louise alone. It works; Louise is happier, feels she can put her hand up without being labelled a 'boff'. No one gets into trouble, and Sara tells me she feels really good about herself for having acted in this way.

Sara embarks on her final year at school in a positive frame of mind. Teachers develop a different view of her and she sees herself as 'reformed' and more mature. She can still be loud at times, but instead of creating confrontational situations by constantly shouting back at staff, she can handle situations assertively.

In one incident she is wrongly accused. Sara tells me, "A few months ago I'd have yelled at the teacher, but I just went to see my Head of Year and he has sorted it out for me."

Karl, Year Eight, has been put in isolation for his own protection because of his inability to refrain from using foul language and insults with all his peers.

In an attempt to focus on a possible area of success in his life I ask him: "Is there anyone that you are never abusive to?"

He doesn't hesitate: "My Grandma."

"I wonder why you are never abusive to her?"

"Because she loves me."

Tracey is in her final year and needs very little support. This case illustrates how a child's feeling of helplessness can lead to aggression and lack of control. Tracey was having outbursts of temper and was being verbally abusive to staff. She frequently walked off site, and would just go home in the middle of the day.

It didn't take long for me to discover that her main problem revolved around anger with her sister Kate. She Kate was in Year Nine and was terrorising Tracey by constantly pulling her hair. Tracey just couldn't cope with her sister at all and bottled up all the anger, because she wasn't allowed to lay a finger on Kate. We talk through the issues and the long and short-term benefit of improved relationships between both girls. I ask her if there is anything she does to support Kate.

"Well, I take her swimming on a Saturday morning."

"I wonder what would happen if you made it on condition she stops pulling your hair.

Tracey smiles. "I think that might work"

It does the trick. Kate stops pulling Tracey's hair and Tracey feels empowered. At school she no longer flares up at the least provocation. She holds down a work experience placement for two weeks and completes her GCSEs.

I have a really vivid dream one night. I find myself in a huge field of long parched brown grasses. As I walk across the field I look down and suddenly see the most vivid red rosebud, no larger than a fingernail. My temptation is to bend down and pluck it, but I sense this is wrong and move on. As I progress through the field I notice there are lots of these tiny buds concealed by the dried stalks.

When I wake I realise the significance of the dream: the buds represent the goodness within each child, and the stalks the problems and difficulties in their lives. Though I want to take each child away from their difficulties and nurture them myself I know that have to leave them where they are. Whatever behaviours they exhibit on the outside each child has a nub of goodness within them. By showing the children unconditional positive regard, without judgement, I can usually find that kernel of goodness and bring it out. What a privilege it is for me to step into their lives and help them along the way.

I wish there was someone outside the family that I could have turned to when I was eight years-old.

A Difficult Time

To set the scene of what was to become a particularly upsetting time for me, and to look at perhaps why it happened, I need to describe one of my older male cousins.

When I was a child of eight, my cousin was around sixteen years-old and a bit of an odd-bod – tall, lanky, and not particularly good looking. He wore thick black glasses and his hair was greasy with Brylcream. At around age twelve he'd had his sticky out ears pinned back, I assume to stop constant bullying. His parents were convinced he would do well in his studies and go on to have a career in a professional field. Oh, how they pushed him. He had to do revision for his exams every night. Unlike Gerald and me, my cousin wasn't allowed to read Superman comics, the *Beano* or the *Dandy*. His leisure times were severely restricted. He had to read 'real' books. He was 'super son' and had a reputation to live up to.

I think it screwed him up. He burst under the pressure and left school at seventeen, never staying to even take his A-Level exams.

My cousin had a baby sister and I used to love my visits to see her.

I am allowed to play with the baby. My aunt always supervises, but today it is different. She tells me she has to go out for a couple of hours. My aunt puts my older cousin in charge.

At first things are fine, but then it is time for the baby's nap. My cousin tells me to go into his bedroom. He is in charge, so I do as I am told. My heart starts to beat a little faster when he locks the door and I am beginning to feel frightened. He unzips his fly and shows me his willy. It is like a fat hairy pink sausage and I don't want to look, but I have to.

He asks me to lift my skirt.

I squirm uncomfortably. He warns me that if I don't do as I am told then I will be in big trouble with the grown ups because I have seen his willy which is rude and it is all my fault.

I believe him.

I lift my skirt and reluctantly allow him to touch me. We hear my aunt's key in the door. She comes straight upstairs and wants to know why the door is locked.

"What have you two been doing?" she demands, her eyes accusatory, her tone furious. Because of her reaction I feel I have done something wrong. I look down and say nothing.

The guilt is overwhelming. If I tell Mum she will be cross. "Why did you let him touch you?" she will ask me. "You knew it was wrong! Why didn't you tell your aunt?"

I know I will never be able to explain, so fear forces my silence.

I suspect my aunt knew my cousin and his habits. How she could possibly have imagined that an eight year-old girl could take any responsibility for that behaviour I fail to comprehend.

The abuse did not stop there. My aunt should have ensured I was never put in such a position again. She didn't. It went on for weeks. I was made to touch my cousin in ways I knew were wrong, the fear of being 'found out' ever greater. I had to suffer the indignities of being touched. Luckily things never went further. I was too terrified to tell my Mum. I kept going over and over what she would say. I knew that it was too late; she would have said, "Why didn't you tell me sooner?"

It wasn't that I thought she wouldn't believe me. I could have told and made it stop but I simply couldn't cope with the guilt. The adult in me can see I *should* have told.

The inner child knows now exactly why I didn't.

This has not been easy for me to write this down – but it is so important that I do. I want to help and protect other children from the guilt that was loaded upon my eight year-old shoulders. It shouldn't have happened.

Looking back, Mum would have been furious with me for not telling, but then I believed she would be furious with me for allowing it to happen... by which time the 'not telling' was far too late.

For years I buried the memories. Not until we covered the topic of sexual abuse in a counselling course forty years later did these memories eventually resurface.

Little Linda (1957)

Diary – 5th October 2007

On Sunday Chris and I cycle to the pub for lunch. I am cautious when I get on my bike. I feel like a novice once more. I wait at all the junctions even if the cars are quite a distance; I don't want to make any sudden movements.

Though we pedal no more than four miles in all it is quite an effort for me. We ride along the coast road to the sound of rigging slapping against the boat masts. In the wind the sound is reminiscent of dissonant church bells. It is good to feel the breeze in my hair and to breathe in the salt air.

I am so grateful I can do this. I dread the onset of treatment, as I know that this will curtail such activity. I try to think positively about it.

Some days I manage, but it is difficult to sustain full time.

Life and Love on Two Wheels

As a small child I often dreamed I was on a two-wheeler bike, perfectly balanced, gliding along at speed, wind in my hair, loving the feeling of self-propulsion.

I begged Mum and Dad for a bike, but they insisted it was way too dangerous, given that we lived in a busy town with lots of traffic. At every opportunity I would ride my friend Rita's large purple trike along the pavement.

Once I was lucky enough to stay for a few days with a friend of the family who had a real two-wheeler. To his Mum's consternation I would not go out with the family on any trips or outings. I spent all my time riding Leon's bike up and down the garden path. I took up proper riding for the first time whilst in my year abroad in Erlangen, West Germany. Groups of us would explore the local countryside, stopping for picnics en route. Returning to Ireland the following year I bought a large-framed secondhand utility bike, which I used for commuting.

It gave me the sense of freedom I had always longed for as a child.

Paul had an aversion to two wheels, so I mostly biked short trips alone during our seventeen years of marriage. Now that I was on my own and the children more independent I was keen to join my the local Cyclists Touring club which organised regular Newcomers Rides from Orpington Station.

In 1991 I set out for the first time on my trusty but heavy five-geared Raleigh to meet with an unknown group of cyclists. I had no idea if I would manage full thirty miles, since I had never ridden more than about sixteen in the past. It took some courage but I presented my self at the station at 10am and quickly got chatting to the other riders. Our leader told us not to worry, as she would take everything at a leisurely pace. We headed towards Shoreham. As we came up the rise we saw a beautiful pink cottage set back from a bridge over a duck pond. It was a stunning view and sold me to the idea of cycle touring. I managed the whole trip without problems and thoroughly enjoyed the experience.

In the following weeks I got to know some of the other cyclists quite well. Much to the amusement of the children, I even began spreading large Ordnance Survey maps out on the lounge floor. Map reading was never a forte of mine. As a child, I had had no exposure to maps in my life, and when my teacher first told us to copy one at primary school I was severely berated for colouring in the sea yellow and the land blue. How was I to understand the difference? Now the motivation was there and I was soon able to find some of the lovelier spots we visited by myself.

I found myself using the Sunday rides as my recreational highlight of the week. I enjoyed the camaraderie of my fellow cyclists, the beauty of the countryside and the freedom to roam around under my own steam listening to the gentle whirring of the wheels beneath.

It was during some of these rides hat I got to know Peter. My Mum and his Dad had died in October 1993, and by the spring of 1994

I found myself spending lots of time talking to him. I knew he was 'safe' as he was married with children so I saw no harm in the friendship.

We spent more and more time with each other until it became clear that there was a magnetism developing between us. He realised too and broke it off eventually, since he felt he was falling in love with me and couldn't trust himself. I felt the loss of his company deeply, but there was no way I would willingly wreck someone else's marriage so I didn't pursue it. Grudgingly, but sensing it was the right thing to do, I let it go, and continued riding on Sundays long after he left the group. He did at least teach me how to love again, and perhaps rekindled a spark in me I thought was long dead after Paul left. I had felt cynical about romance and my self-esteem had taken a huge battering. Peter taught me that I was a worthwhile person and that I needed to believe in myself.

After some months with the club it became clear that we Newcomers were not Newcomers any more and a group of about six of us became really good friends. Chris, dark haired, blue eyed, bearded, Lycra-clad and enigmatic became a regular, and he and I got on very well. We decided between us to form a new group. Four years after that first ride the new section was formed, The Intermediates. It became very popular, as we were a friendly bunch of people who always welcomed new faces.

Each week Chris would use his powers of persuasion to recruit potential leaders. This wasn't always successful, and one time the response from a particularly reluctant rider was strident in its protest: "Me? No way! I just concentrate on the bum in front."

Our rides were normally interspersed with tea and lunch stops, which frequently generated esoteric discussions.

Ted related a recent article he had read about headaches and how they can sometimes be an early indicator of heart trouble.

"I get a headache after four pints," he announced. Needless to say none of us volunteered to telephone for an ambulance.

Discussing the relative differences between mounting a penny-farthing and a horse one day, Sue provided this pertinent insight: "At least with a penny-farthing it won't suddenly drop its head and begin eating grass."

Occasionally these discussions would revolve around food, Chris' idea of a healthy diet being a six pack of doughnuts or a giant bar of chocolate, where Jane preferred MacDonalds and chips, but only on Sundays.

I did try to re-educate Chris' palate many times. "What did you have for breakfast?"

"Chocolate," he would say.

"Toast would be a healthier option."

"Yes, but it doesn't taste as good."

We met some characters on some of our rides. Phil attempted a demonstration of how to fell an attacker in ten easy lessons – or maybe it was one easy lesson, it just seemed like ten by the time he had finished!

His repartee was doomed to failure as he whispered alluringly in Geraldine's ear, "Could I put my hands around your neck please?"

Phil's credibility came under serious threat when he hitched up his leggings and proudly announced, "These aren't cycling tights you know, they are really ballet trousers."

It is sometimes difficult to hold conversations that flow when cycling in a group, but one visitor from the Hull and East Riding section informed us as to how its done by citing an example of one of their local cyclists, "She ad two sets o' lungs – one for climbin t' hills, and t'other for yakking."

After one particularly foggy and icy ride to the Christmas sing-song, Simon (who had regaled us with tales of his African tour) was sporting a neck collar.

"Did you do that in Africa?" asked his friend, overcome with admiration.

"Oh this... no I ricked my neck last night, drying my hair."

We overheard Debbie relating this strange tale: "Well she was looking forward to a nice boiled egg, but then as the water heated up it hatched..."

In the spring of 1996, the Intermediates went on the first of many cycle tours to Bruges. What I loved about this and other tours was the freedom of being abroad and cycling along beautiful tracks rather than clogged up roads. I enjoyed the company, the ambiance and the wealth of new experiences.

Everyone assumed that Chris and I were more than good friends despite our stringent denials. It didn't help when we both turned up late at the station one Sunday; me because of a puncture, and Chris because of his poor time keeping! We made our way to Westerham for the elevenses stop and when we arrived at the café everyone was exchanging knowing looks. We knew how it must have appeared, but no one believed our story.

I had been so pre-occupied with Peter initially that I hadn't really noticed Chris. Then I felt he was wasn't interested, and turned my attention to other friendships. At this point Chris realised that another man was taking more than a passing interest in me and he was nervous of losing a good female friend. We started spending more time together. When we did finally get together just a few short weeks later we were slightly embarrassed and chose to keep it a secret for ages. Perhaps others could see what we were missing ourselves. We were two lonely souls who craved intimacy, yet found it difficult to play the usual 'games'. Chris was depressed having had strong feelings for another woman that were not reciprocated. I felt sorry for him, and as he revealed his emotions to me, I responded. I had always found him physically attractive.

It wasn't easy to start a new relationship. I was terrified of rejection and my self-esteem was still a little low. We started going out together and gelled really well, to the point where we even discussed moving in with each other. Chris was loving, gentle and supportive. We began playing guitar together which bonded us, as I could see the fervour with which he played his bass. He has a real feel for music. We had romantic cycle trips in bathed in the golden light of the late summer sun, lots of fun and laughter. Being with him always lifted my spirits and made work seem a million miles away. If I did have work-related problems, Chris would listen attentively and offer advice. Things were going really smoothly.

It was Rachel's eighteenth birthday party and she wanted me out of the house, so the plan was for me to stay in the flat with Chris overnight. Chris was telling me with his words that he loved me and wanted to be with me, but that night I was beginning to receive mixed messages when he began hypothesising about what he would do if the woman he had previously been in love with began to respond. He also told me that another woman had made a pass at him, and asked me how hurt I would be if he went along with it.

I did some serious thinking after that and wrote him a letter in which I made it very clear that I felt I was worth more.

I finished the letter:

> *I think what I am saying is that in my heart I can't continue a fantasy relationship. I have very strong feelings for you and I don't want to lose your friendship, but perhaps while things are so unsettled in your mind it would be fairer to both of us just to revert back to our friendship. I think that is still possible. My wounds from the last relationship are too sore to face this kind of pain again. I'm not accusing you of anything. I don't blame you. I just can't go on with this uncertainty… when I know that you make love with your body, but your heart is with someone else and your mind is possibly even with a third person.*
>
> *So I am not asking you to make a choice because I recognise that your aren't able to do that. So I am making the choice;*

it is just as much my choice to make; and when we come together on Wednesday to talk, then perhaps this letter can be a starting point and you now know in advance part of what I feel and you will have had the time to think about it.

Having written that, and put it through his door I began to agonise over everything.

I had no doubt that until now it was the best relationship I had ever experienced. We were calm and always listened to each other. Chris was sensitive and empathic. We had great fun and I loved his company… but ultimately I knew that would not be enough. I recognised I was worth more than being 'second best'.

I concluded after my musings that I would give him an ultimatum. If the past few months together hadn't changed his feelings then our relationship was nothing more than a fantasy.

When Paul divorced me, when Peter broke off our liaison, I was given no say in the outcome. This time I was determined things would be different. I knew that I had been alone for ten years and that one is an okay number. I had loved being a couple again, but the pairing had to be meaningful for both of us. I prepared myself mentally and emotionally for a break-up. I knew I had been down that hole before. This time I would climb back out unaided.

In one strange call from Chris on the Sunday he said he wouldn't be out on the ride. I didn't question it.

For two days I heard nothing and had resigned myself to the fact that this was the end. Chris rang on the Tuesday. He told me how sorry he was to have hurt me. He had regretted his words and had needed time to think things through.

"You are really important to me, and I don't want to loose you. Your letter shocked me, but in a way it was a good thing. I realise the depth of your feeling now. Sometimes you don't respond when I say I love you. Now I realise you do. I am sorry but I just wasn't ready to talk on Sunday."

"Maybe not, but I was. I should have told you at the time, 'This can't wait'. I'm not sure why I didn't."

We met up and talked about it all for hours. Ultimately it put our relationship on a much stronger footing. When I went for a new job by the sea on the Isle of Wight, Chris and I made a commitment to set up home together. Five years later we married. Like any couple we have had our ups and downs, but we have a special relationship and love each other dearly.

Diary – 9th October 2007

As the days lead up to the first chemotherapy session I feel like the condemned prisoner enjoying the last few meals. I feel physically much stronger now, and am loving the freedom of relaxed days, yet the thought of what is to come looms threateningly.

I speak to Jonathan on the phone about the trial drug. He has been wonderful through this and gives me sound advice. He is a doctor, and has spoken to colleagues about the cancer. He suggests that if my chances are more than eighty percent it wouldn't be worth having the additional drug. If much lower, then I should go for it if that is what I want. I really appreciate his support.

I still struggle to find meaning in what is happening to me. I don't like the thought of being dependant on the hospital for my survival. It sits really uncomfortably with me and throws up difficult memories.

The Hospital

The room was unchanged; the pink floral curtain round the bed, the oxygen cylinder in the corner, the hospital sink, the obligatory jug of water. I turned to look at the frail figure in the bed. He was lying flat for the first time. Only yesterday he'd been sitting up, fighting sleep, fighting death, shouting out irrational orders.

"Fetch me a drink from the fridge!"

"There isn't a fridge, Dad. You're in the hospital," I responded calmly, hoping to re-orientate him. The effect was momentary.

"Go on, do as you're told! Get me some orange."

He'd wave his hand vaguely in the air seeing a world beyond the bare magnolia walls. Gentler now, almost pleading, he added, "I've had enough of this party. It's too noisy. Take me up to the flat. Go on. We can go up in the lift."

Dad became agitated when I wouldn't comply with his increasingly bizarre requests. I'd had to choke back my tears.

Now he was just lying there looking exhausted.

"Is he ok?" I asked the agency nurse.

"He's alright," came the reply.

"He doesn't sound alright. He's struggling to breathe."

The agency recruit seemed unmoved.

"You wouldn't let a dog suffer like this," I thought angrily, but lacked the courage to utter the words aloud.

Suddenly Dad's eyelids flickered and he rasped, "Fetch the doctor!"

I could see that it terrified him to let go. I ran out to the nurse's station somehow summoning the courage to interrupt the Charge Nurse's phone call.

"Please come quickly! He can't breathe!" My flash of assertiveness surprised me.

Maddeningly calm, the Charge Nurse strode into the side room.

"Could you wait outside?" he asked me. "I think we can make him more comfortable."

Shut out of the room I allowed my thoughts to drift back to Dad's warden-assisted flat, where I was temporarily staying.

It seemed strangely different without him. The bathroom was rank with urine. It was so unlike my father, who had been fastidious when he was well. The flat was spartan in comparison with the homely mess at Ardwell Avenue when Mum was alive.

"Oh, don't throw that away, " She would plead. "It's A YNK – You Never Know when you might need it!"

Once I opened a cupboard and box after box of toothpicks tumbled out. When I asked why she had so many she simply looked at me with a meek, "You Never Know…."

I did know that there were enough for at least two lifetimes.

Looking round the bedroom in the flat, I had a momentary shock seeing Dad's hairpiece on a stand. He'd insisted on wearing one in the hospital though it looked ridiculous forced into a rakish angle by the pillow. Proud of his good looks my father had had several girlfriends after Mum died. None, however, lasted for long.

"Dad, what happened to Eve?"

"I ditched her."

"Why? She was nice."

"She was too old for me," he grunted, dismissively.

"How old was she?"

"Seventy-eight."

"But Dad you're going on eighty-two yourself!"

The opening door broke my reverie. Invited back into the room I saw that Dad had slipped into a coma, a nebuliser over his face, each breath sending a coil of white mist into the air.

I looked at the Charge Nurse. "How long?"

He shrugged. Why couldn't they ever be honest? The agency nurse still sat there detached and uncaring. I half expected her to start knitting. My withering look was wasted on her.

Dad's breath became increasingly shallow. There was a long deep sigh, and his skin turned waxen.

And so it was that on Thursday 24th July 2002 Dad took his last breath.

It signalled a merciful release – for both of us.

Diary – 11th October 2007

Today I have a shock when we see Dr B. I had the routine blood test first and was expecting only to discuss the trial drug and whether or not I wanted to be considered for it.

Then the bombshell:

"I do apologise. I mis-spelt your name and as a result haven't had a chance to discuss your recent detailed scans with the liver surgeons. The tumours may not be operable, in which case we are speaking only of palliative care. I should have an answer for you in about half an hour, if you'd like to come back then."

Chris and I go for a cup of tea. I am numb with shock. Do I prepare myself to die? Do I insist on a second opinion… what the hell do I do?

In the café I go through the motions of drinking. It is like seeing the world through distorted glasses. Everything feels weird, different as though I am detached. How do I deal with this? Chris can't speak. His eyes say it all.

We return in silence. We wait no more than five minutes and are taken into one of the side rooms.

"They have decided that you are borderline operable. One of the tumours is close to a crucial blood vessel, which means that it could be dangerous to operate. We are hoping the chemo will shrink it down sufficiently."

I ask him what my statistical chances are. They are no higher than forty to fifty percent. On that basis I opt to be part of the trial drug. It means weekly hospital visits, skin rashes and acne. I feel there is little alternative. The research nurse explains that only fifty percent of accepted patients receive the drug, though everyone on the trial is carefully monitored. She promises to ring later and let me know the outcome.

When we get home there is an answer phone message. I am to have the new drug starting next week.

Chris and I could not have foreseen any of this when we married in 2005. If we had, would either of us have gone ahead with the wedding?

The Wedding

It has always been frowned upon for a Jew to marry a non-Jew, and had I not looked on Genes Reunited I would never have found out that Fanny Barwell had been ostracised by the family and had killed herself in such tragic circumstances because of a mixed marriage. Grandma had a brother who also 'married out'. His name was Henry. Henry's daughter Pat only realised years later about the other half of her family being Jewish.

Mum always discouraged me from going out with non-Jewish boys but once at university that never really stopped me. I suppose deep down I couldn't see the difference. Maybe it was feeling that pressure that finally pushed me into marrying in the faith. I believed that I loved Paul at the time, but I may have just been in love with the idea of love.

Mum and Dad's attitude did change over the years. They had two children, who both married Jewish partners and both relationships ended in disaster. When Gerald was in hospital having his leg amputated at age thirty-three, his wife was sleeping with another man. Paul fell in love with a younger woman after seventeen years of marriage with me. Perhaps that's what changed their minds. Mum never met Chris, but I know in my heart of hearts she would have admired and liked him because he treats me with such great respect and love.

The day of our wedding dawned like a page from a fairy tale. I looked out the window at around six-thirty to see the sun casting its warm fresh golden light across the water. I rose and made my way down to the beach for an early morning swim. It was idyllic. With each stroke I thought of our relationship and how happy I was deep inside. Refreshed and ready to face the day I returned to the house for a shower and some breakfast. Rachel, Jonathan, Levana and Ziva were staying with us. Chris was with his relatives in a Newport Hotel.

Chris had arranged a horse-and-carriage to take us to the venue, Haseley Manor, a stunning mediaeval manor house in a magnificent setting. Rachel, Levana and I arrived in style! We wanted the day to be a really happy occasion.

When I first met Chris' family I realised why he was such a loving person. They have always made me feel part of the family. I think they were worried at first that they might frighten me off because of their off-beat sense of humour. It just made me feel as though it was home from home.

I was thrilled to be marrying Chris. After my divorce in 1991 I went through a few frogs looking for my prince. I gave most dates what I called 'the fridge test'. It was how I measured whether or not I was having a good time. I would ask myself, "Am I really liking this or would I rather be at home cleaning the fridge?"

Chris passed the fridge test. I had finally found my prince.

We didn't ask for any wedding gifts, as we felt that after five years in the house we had all we needed. There was, however, one thing that Chris and I particularly wanted. It was a new bed. We couldn't really ask for one from any of our guests, so we were resigned to just buying one. My Mum and Dad did not live long enough to see our wedding day, but ironically, on my birthday that year, a cheque came through the post. It was from the solicitor, and came very late, but it was to do with the remainder of Dad's estate. The amount was exactly enough to buy the bed. I saw it as their gift to us, from beyond the grave.

We ate, drank, laughed, strolled round the grounds, spoke at length to friends and family and danced together later in the evening to a live band.

28th August 2005 was a day to remember.

Diary – 14th October 2007

Looking out of the window this morning I see a break in the successive days of grey gloom. The sun is shining in a vivid blue sky.

I am motivated to try a longer walk than usual, so Chris and I make our way along the marshes towards Bembridge. From there we continue along the coastline heading for the lifeboat station. The views are stunning. A few dog walkers roam the beach but it is otherwise calm and undisturbed. Waves chase each other in formation, coming to shore sideways like green combs through curly grey hair. The sunshine is watery but warm. As we walk along by the sea our feet sink deeply into the damp sand. It feels as though we are trudging through a giant marshmallow. Occasionally we must scrabble over rocks and groins to avoid the tide.

I enjoy each moment, savouring the smells sights and sounds. Chris and I chatter as we walk, and the topic of male friends comes up.

I tell him some of the stories I remember from my student days.

Boyfriends

Malcolm was tall, gangly with sticky-out ears, and he absolutely adored me. At first I was flattered to be the object of such attention, but gradually the novelty wore off. I didn't mind his looks, but he was so serious it didn't suit my personality at all. He would moon over me endlessly, telling me how much he loved me. I just couldn't reciprocate.

After a few weeks I was desperate to break it off, but didn't quite know how. One evening at my house Malcolm was sitting in the front room holding my hand. He suddenly said, "You know I love you so much if you leave me I will kill myself."

Bearing in mind I was barely fifteen, I really couldn't handle the drama. I wasn't sure what to do. We were moving from Stratford to

Barkingside, so I just didn't give him the new address or indeed tell him I was leaving the area. I felt bad about it afterwards, but it seemed the only way to manage the situation. I often wonder how he reacted when he found out.

Mum and Dad were very protective of me as far as boys were concerned, so I had all the usual warnings. During my university year in Germany I had my share of boyfriends, but what I vividly remember was an arrangement I wanted to make with a fellow student with whom I was not romantically involved. I was due home for the summer break and one of the Theology students who had a girlfriend in Scotland was making the trip to England in his car. He suggested a car share, and I was delighted. It was a cheap way for me to return to the UK.

I rang Mum and told her.

"Oh no, you can't possibly share a car with a male student. You hardly know him. He could rape you."

At this point I started laughing. "No Mum, you don't understand. He has a girlfriend. He is not remotely interested in me. Besides he is six feet four and like a beanpole. He really isn't my type at all. He is studying the Bible. His mind is on other things I promise you."

Mum was still worried and I could hear Dad chuntering in the background: "No absolutely not. Very dangerous." I could visualise his disapproving pout and shake of the head.

Eventually, convinced that Theo really did have a girlfriend in Scotland, they reluctantly agreed to my making the journey on the understanding that Theo would spend one night at our house before making his way on to Scotland.

We arrived as arranged and Dad opened the door. I saw his eyes move from Theo's size twelve feet, up his long thin body to his thick black-rimmed glasses and acne-pitted face. Dad moved quickly into the lounge hiding his enormous grin in a handkerchief and pretending to blow his nose. It was probably relief that my description had been so accurate.

Theo spoke not a word of English so that evening at dinner I was translating from English into German for Theo, and back again for Mum and Dad. Half way through the meal Mum looked at me blankly. I realised I'd unwittingly spoken to her in German!

I think my parents trusted my judgement a little more after that episode.

Patrick was good-looking which attracted me to him in the first place. He had deep blue eyes and a neatly chiselled nose. He was Swiss, so my French came on a treat while I went out with him. He had come to the university as the French Language assistant and we had a fun relationship. A few months on I began to have doubts. He invited me to Geneva for three weeks to stay in the apartment with his Mum and Dad. That was when I realised that the Swiss do things differently regarding personal hygiene. His mum did the laundry carefully just once a week, which was the only time Patrick wore clean clothes, and by then I felt he was a bit whiffy.

Like several previous boyfriends, Patrick was hooked on me and when he had to return to Switzerland at the end of the year and I went to Erlangen he wrote me long passionate screeds declaring his undying love. I probably would have backed off at that point, except Mum's total resistance to the idea of me getting hitched to a non-Jew. It was a no-no, and it made me rebel against her wishes. Had she been okay with the concept I would probably have broken it off with Patrick a lot earlier. As it was I carried on writing to him until I met Tom in the first couple of weeks in Erlangen.

Tom was the first romantic encounter where the feelings we had for each other were entirely reciprocated. I fell for his chat up line "Did anyone tell you you have lovely thumbs?" and for his remarkably dark brown eyes and handsomely rugged features. He was of Greek extraction and it showed in his undeniably good looks. His beard was an added attraction to me.

Tom had come to Erlangen as a GI, and then gone on to study at the university. The physical bond between us was strong, and we hit it off together, sharing the same wicked sense of humour. We laughed together, ate together and had huge amounts of fun. One time we went on a ski trip in the Austrian Alps. The only way they would allow us to share a room was if we were married (how times have changed) so Tom brought his GI papers which looked official, and banked on the fact that the grey-haired old Austrian landlady couldn't read English. He was right. So with a cheap fake ring we had a splendid week on the slopes. I had never skied and was too afraid to try, but I went ice-skating and walking in the mountains. It was a wonderful holiday and I savoured the complete experience, the peace and the beauty of the magnificent Austrian Alps.

One evening we had been walking up a mountain and Tom was worried we wouldn't make it down before dark. He broke off a piece of wood from a tree and we used it as a makeshift toboggan. It did the trick, but when we turned it over at the bottom we realised it said 'red run'. We had bumped our way down a steep and dangerous ski run! Crazy. Oh the madness of youth! Tom encouraged me to ride a bike. I used to sit on the back of his bike to get used to balancing again, and the German police would shout after us 'Absteigen! Absteigen!' as it was against the law to be two on a bike. Of course we pretended not to understand the language, but they probably saw through our trick.

Tom wanted to marry me, of course. He proposed many times and wrote me the most beautiful romantic poetry. He also encouraged me to use my writing skills. I might have been tempted; but one time during my Erlangen stay I went to my friend Sabine for three weeks in Lübeck. In that time Tom had a fling with another woman. I realised in time that probably because of his good looks he would be a bit of a womaniser. If I couldn't trust him after six months, how could I trust him in a marriage?

Though it broke my heart I knew I couldn't marry him. I terminated the relationship.

Diary – 15th October 2007

Today I have the appointment in the Chemo Unit, which prepares me for Friday when I must expect to spend the whole day with them.

The nurse leads us into a private office and we sit at a large wooden table. First I have to answer questions about my current state of health to compare in a few weeks time. The questions are a clear indicator of what I am to expect. Do I have mouth ulcers/conjunctivitis/eczema/breathing problems/diarrhoea/nausea/vomiting? The nurse tells us when to call an ambulance. It is daunting. I may experience a crushing pain in my chest or tightness in my throat triggered by cold, that stops me breathing. If I have the beginnings of an infection I am to notify them immediately.

The nurse warns me about other symptoms I can't ignore. My hands and feet could swell which might precede all the skin peeling off; highly dangerous…

If I was scared before, it's now right off the scale.

I am entering new territory and I have no map.

New Location

When I was in my early thirties I had a dream that left an indelible imprint in my mind. I was living in a house, which overlooked a pebble beach and harbour. Each day I could open the patio door and walk down to the sea. Everything in the dream was vivid. The multi coloured pebbles, the red and blue sails on the boat, the tide lapping against the shoreline, the smell of the salt air. The dream fired a longing to live by the sea that never left me.

After four years working in Behaviour Support the little voice in my head that I had learned to listen to started prodding me. "You don't have to live in this busy place any more. Why not move to the coast?"

I was no longer comfortable living in Orpington. The roads were becoming increasingly clogged with traffic and my desire to live by the sea was ever stronger. There was now very little chaining me to this area. I started to look half-heartedly at jobs near the coast, but inertia may have prevented me from moving if things hadn't come to a head around Christmas 1998.

I had one horrific shopping trip to the supermarket, which nearly sent me over the top. The traffic was bad, which was to be expected on a Friday night. Then a silver Micra pulled out in front of me the driver determined not to increase speed beyond twenty miles per hour, foot almost permanently on the brake.

As I joined the line of cars for the Superstore I realised my jaw was aching from clenched teeth. Fifteen minutes in the queue and I was seething with frustration, tired after a day at work and just desperate to get home. I tussled with a red Peugeot for the last bay in car park six, silently cursing the Christmas season. All I wanted was to do the week's shopping.

I grabbed the bags from the boot of the car and crossed over to the entrance dodging through the lines of traffic, trying to avoid breathing the petrol fumes which hung persistently on the cold evening air. What a day! Now there were no trolleys left, forcing another delay. At last I pounced on a free trolley and was glad when the entry doors, like curtains, closed out the bitingly cold wind. I patrolled the shelves mentally ticking off the items I needed. Most of the goods had been re-arranged to accommodate the Christmas biscuits and treats, adding to my frustrations. I persevered, yanking my obstinate trolley from aisle to aisle.

Finally I struggled over to the checkout to pick the optimum queue. Ten minutes on and I realised the queue wasn't moving at all. Why? At the front was a lady with a fistful of rejected coupons, protesting to the checkout staff. The cashier rang her bell for assistance. I looked frantically round for a response. I sensed my face flushing with heat and anger and knew that any second I would either scream hysterically or walk out of the supermarket abandoning my shopping and my dignity.

Then a woman's voice, cracked and unsteady saved the moment: "I only come in for a bit o' fish!"

I turned to see a frail elderly lady with a baffled expression on her creased face.

Magic. It brought a smile to my lips. The old lady in the green baize coat showed her basket. Poking out from the top was a solitary piece of fish wrapped in paper. This woman had been queuing for the best part of twenty minutes for her one meagre purchase. I found myself focusing full attention on the woman's sorry tale.

"See, I don't live local. I caught the bus in. I don't know what's happened to the service lately. Had to wait half an hour I did… and then it was stop-start nearly all the way. D'you know I left the house just after four? And now this!" The old lady gave an exasperated glance in the direction of the checkout girl who was still waiting for the supervisor. "I wish I hadn't bothered."

"Go on, you go first," I found myself saying as we reached the till.

Once outside I recognised the green baize coat in the distance. The old lady sat huddled at the bus stop, her fish just visible from the bag on the bench beside her. There was no sign of a bus.

Before I could stop myself I had crossed over the pedestrian walkway and the words were out. "Where do you live?"

"Sidcup."

"Want a lift?"

I didn't quite know what came over me but I was totally unable to fight the urge to repay this old woman by helping her get home. She had single-handedly lifted my toxic mood.

"Are you sure? Isn't it out of your way?"

"Doesn't really matter." I assured her. "I'm in no hurry!"

Forty minutes later as I waved goodbye to my unexpected guest I drove home, arriving much later than planned but feeling resolute. As well as helping me through a difficult moment the encounter with the old lady helped me to clarify my thoughts. It was clear to me that I couldn't carry on with these stress levels. I was determined to find a job in a new, less crowded location.

About a year later, I saw a post advertised at Carisbrooke High School on the Isle of Wight, which looked really appealing. They wanted someone to help set up a Behaviour Support Centre within the mainstream school.

I was called for interview just before the February half term, 2000. Chris and I travelled over to the Island together and stayed overnight near Newport Quay. Whilst I was at interview Chris visited some estate agents to preview houses in Newport. We agreed to meet up late afternoon in the hotel. I felt that my experience in Behaviour Support made me a strong candidate for the post. Clearly the panel agreed since they offered me the job. I was delighted.

We spent the weekend looking at houses and it was a real wrench having to return to Orpington. We loved the Island and it felt like exactly the right move for us both.

A few days later some estate agent details came through the post and one of them in particular caught my eye. It was a newly built house, which was just a five-minute walk from the harbour.

The following week Chris and I went to see it. As soon as we got off the bus we realised that the location was perfect. Just as had happened with Sparrow Drive I had a strong feeling that it was a comfortable road and exactly the right house. There was no flooring and aside from the kitchen the place was an empty shell; but so much potential. We could picture an ensuite in the huge upstairs bedroom and tiles on the floors downstairs. The place was affordable; this was it!

Once we had looked around the property we explored the harbour and causeway. After a short ten-minute stroll across the Duver I saw some beach huts in the distance.

"That's the sea," Chris said, "just behind those huts."

I started to run. I couldn't believe that I had a chance of living so close to the coast. I would be able to swim all through the summer. It was a dream come true.

First I had to sell the town house in Orpington. Compared with the stresses of selling the Cobden Road property, this went extremely smoothly. I was lucky enough to get an offer from a property developer who was a cash buyer. No chain either end!

The whole process took less than six weeks, and in April 2000 we moved to the Island. I began my job at the beginning of the spring term in May. It was perfect timing.

Diary – 18th October 2007

It creeps closer. I am counting the days. In the night I dream I am all alone in a dinghy, which suddenly propels itself away from the shore over shallow water full of rocks and dangerous obstacles. I feel totally helpless. I am unable to steer it, and can only move slightly here and there to stop the boat puncturing. I relate the dream to Chris. We can both see that it is a metaphor for my impending treatment.

This evening Chris and I watch the DVD about the chemo tablets. It doesn't have the excitement of Star Trek *and the only dynamic bit is when the presenter rises from the garden chair and walks past a water fountain. If it is supposed to help me feel calm and serene it is a let down. It is more reminiscent of a mind-numbingly dull late night Open University lecture from the Eighties.*

My bag is packed in readiness. Tomorrow is the big day. I've to be there at ten thirty. It is out of my hands now.

The driver organised by the local Cancer Trust comes to the house a little early. When we arrive at the Chemo suite at 10.20am it looks more like a beauty parlour than a hospital! I half expect to see a nail bar in the corner. The tasteful colour scheme is a vivid combination of green yellow and purple. Artistically designed glass mobiles are suspended from the ceiling.

The nurse comes round with the pre-med, which is a mix of Paracetamol, a steroid and an anti sickness drug. The canula goes in easily following the application of a warming pad. For the first two hours I receive an infusion of the trial antibody. They take observations every fifteen minutes initially. I am not worried about this drug, as I know the side effects shouldn't kick in too dramatically.

Not until late afternoon do they give me the dreaded Oxaliplatin. My arm aches a little for an hour and a half, but in the last thirty minutes it feels as though acid is being fed into my vein. My arm is excruciatingly painful. My nerves are now hypersensitive to cold and I can't touch even the zip on my trousers without this uncomfortable tingling sensation, like an electric shock.

They finally release me at 5.30pm. At home I have to rethink the simplest everyday activities like going to the fridge or turning on a tap. Putting on a glove first helps, but I feel like an alien creature.

I remember once opening the fridge door and having a terrible shock. In the door rack I saw six dark green hairy eggs and immediately thought we'd been invaded by creatures from outer space. It was simply that Paul had thought the egg rack a great place to store kiwi fruit. Sometimes my imagination goes to overdrive.

The side effects of the treatment are brutally evident to me now, but at least I have conquered my fear. I know what it is I am facing, which helps quite a bit. I remember how I felt after splitting up with Paul following seventeen years of marriage. To be all alone after so long was a daunting prospect.

Going solo

I decided to set myself a challenge to prove I could enjoy a holiday as a single person. Since I enjoyed cycling so much it wasn't a difficult choice and I picked a week's camping holiday in Wales. It looked interesting, and stress free. I didn't even have to take my own tent. Breakfast and evening meal were provided on site, and lunches were midday stops en route. The campsite had full facilities including showers and toilets. The mileage was manageable, between twenty and forty per day, though I was aware the terrain was hilly.

My biggest fear was that no one would talk to me and I would absolutely hate it. I made up my mind that if the holiday was awful and turned out like that I would simply drive my car home again. Sorted. Nothing would force me to stay. Knowing I had this 'get out' clause helped me be brave.

First I had to navigate the route. Dad was helpful in that he got written instructions from the AA, which had a map plus details of motorways, junctions, etc. Armed with this I set out from Orpington one fine August morning in my VW and headed for Erwood near the Herefordshire borders. The campsite was a remote field in the country. The organisers had arranged a 'getting to know you' session for the first evening, and everyone was amazingly warm and friendly. On the first night I asked if I should lock my bike. Everyone laughed at me, since our only intruders were likely to be Welsh sheep. A group of us walked to the pub later in the evening but forgot how dark Wales can be. On the way back we had to link arms to navigate our path in the pitch black. We could see nothing whatsoever and we had to poke around in the campsite once we did return to identify our tents until someone managed to find a torch.

Each night I slept like a log, warm and cosy in the tent. It was so quiet. We showered in small cubicles looking out onto the beautiful countryside.

I heard a couple of women speaking German, and introduced myself. It turned out that Andrea was married to someone called Peter. He was Bine's brother – my German exchange partner at school whom I'd kept in touch with all those years. She'd had the info about the holiday from Bine, because I'd sent it! Andrea and I became firm friends and even arranged a school exchange together.

That holiday was liberating for me in many ways. It helped me to realise that I could choose the people I wanted to spend time with and that I could enjoy myself without a partner. It took courage to take up the challenge of the holiday, but it was worth it.

Diary – 22nd October 2007

Another strange dream last night. I was trying to travel somewhere with a group of people but each time we came to the end of the road there was an ambush waiting. Soldiers with guns. I had to move fast in the opposite direction. This repeated itself several times. I kept forgetting about the troops and fell into the trap time and again. It was frustrating.

Thinking about it I wondered if it was my difficulty in facing the side effects of the treatment. I keep trying to pursue my life, but come across these barriers to normal functioning.

Yesterday I tried going out on the bike. Despite the protection of gloves the pins and needles became intense. I stopped at the shop to buy a few things but couldn't move my hands even to lock up the bike. In the supermarket it was agony just putting things into the basket. Then I came to the check out. I felt clumsy as I shakily attempted to extract a ten pound note from a purse that was evading my grip. For someone who has always looked young for her age it is so difficult to feel old and doddery.

This is the lady who was told off for going up the staff staircase in her first job. And on a day trip with the family to the fairground I was warned, "No, you can't use the go kart track. You have to be twelve years-old." I was thirty-four at the time and when I took off my hood and showed the cashier my wedding ring he was duly admonished! The children thought it hilarious.

When Rachel was about three, a salesman knocked on my door. I opened it to be greeted by the question: "Is your Mummy in?" I was so embarrassed I didn't have the wherewithal to respond with a nonchalant, "No, but my daughter is!" so I just closed the door.

Daniel has come to stay for a few days as he has half term. I watch him make a pumpkin pie in the kitchen. I have to go upstairs to lie down for half an hour as I feel nauseous, but fortunately by tea-time I am recovered enough to try some.

Dan really lifts my spirits and makes me laugh. When I am with him it is hard to believe that there is anything wrong with me.

This morning Dan is returning to Leeds. I wake up with the predicted skin rash. It burns and itches. I look in the mirror at the unsightly eruptions in my normally clear skin. Will it reach the point where I need a paper bag over my head before I can leave the house? I resemble a Star Trek *alien who has contracted Freighter Blight. Maybe tomorrow I will waken with the notorious forehead ridges and speaking fluent Klingon.*

Hopefully I will see Dan again at Christmas, but what state will I be in by then? Can I really sustain this for six months?

Today I go for my second session with the trial drug. I have a chat with the research nurse, Minna, who reminds me of a vampire victim. She has a Transylvanian accent and looks terribly pale. Wasn't Minna Harker one of Dracula's unfortunates?

Minna tells me that the neuropathy should not last for much more than a week and if it is still bad in a fortnight's time they will lower the Oxaliplatin dosage. That is a relief. It is really important for me to maintain my every day activities. I am at the hospital longer than planned as my veins are initially in rebellious mode.

I am mortified when I get home. Not over the chemo, or the cancer. I have left my watch on the bedside table. Bizarre.

27th October

Bad night last night. Probably the steroid injection. I woke at two thirty and didn't go back to sleep.

Today is fairly mild, so Chris and I decide to cycle into Ryde. It is my first trip over two miles since treatment started. I wear silk gloves and mittens over. Fortunately the neuropathy is nowhere near as severe and it is pleasant enough, marred only by my irrational anger at anyone who blocks my path, steps in front of me, or pulls out in a car without looking. Intellect tells me I have to let such behaviour go. I am only hurting myself by becoming stressed. Chris can see that I am not coping with these incidents and tries to talk to me, but the more effort I make at controlling the emotional surges, the harder it becomes.

When we get home, we talk it through. I think the issue is my needing to recognise that I am perhaps not dealing with this treatment programme and with the acceptance of the illness as well as it appears on the surface. Everyone at the hospital sees the cheerful stoical me. As a result my anger is mis-directed. What do I do about it? I need to take myself in hand, but how? Sometimes I feel like I am going mad.

Perhaps I have inherited my temper from my Dad.

Dad's Temper

In the Fifties and Sixties it was common for parents to smack children if they were naughty. Dad had amateur boxing medals along with a terrible temper. Mum always made it clear that Dad was never allowed to smack us.

Like any teenager I was a bit lippy at times. One day I was particularly cheeky to the caretaker at the local Synagogue. At the end of his tether with a whole group of us the caretaker reacted to my rudeness by slapping me round the face. Instinctively I found the courage to aim a big kick at his shin, which was all I could reach at the time given that he was about six feet tall. I confessed to Mum as soon as I got in.

"You shouldn't have been rude," she said, "but he had no right to hit you. Whatever you do, don't tell your father!"

"Why not?"

"Because he's sure to give him what for! Best say nothing!"

I don't recall how Dad found out. Mum told me the next day. "The caretaker has been sacked."

"What happened?"

"Dad went up there this evening. He asked the caretaker if he'd hit you. The caretaker admitted it but then he had the cheek to roll up his trouser leg point to a whopping great bruise and plead, 'But look what she did to me'!"

"What did Dad say?"

"He warned him, 'Don't you ever lay a finger on my daughter again!' punched him hard, and the blow laid the caretaker right out! He's lost his job for hitting you."

Only once was I ever on the receiving end of that temper. Gerald and Dad were constantly arguing. Perhaps they were too similar in nature, impatient and hot-headed. Gerald at sixteen thought he knew everything and that Dad knew nothing. There was so much yelling every night at the dinner table it was unsettling. Mum once threatened divorce because Dad insisted Gerald should leave home. Maybe some of the stress and tension had rubbed off onto me.

One Saturday when Mum was at work I was just needling Dad constantly. I went too far and he lost it with me. Mum was out. He chased me up the stairs. He really laid into me, punching and pummelling me where I lay on the bed. I was bruised and smarting for hours afterwards. I sobbed into my pillow for ages. I kept the beating a secret from Mum. I knew that the only rift between my parents was over us children. Mum never found out. The isolated incident was never mentioned, by either of us. Mum clearly had the insight to realise Dad's temper was out of control.

Diary – 28th October 2007

The clocks went back last night. Now that I am not working it doesn't seem important to me any more. I had another odd dream. I was in a house where builders were embarking on a major refurbishment. There were lots of loose floorboards and I was warned to tread extremely carefully as they were being replaced. I felt optimistic in the dream as though the disruption and chaos would be worth it in the longer term.

I hope it is my subconscious looking positively at the Cancer treatment. I know that others see me as a very strong person who will be able to face this unknown bravely. I am not convinced they are right, and yet I have always been willing to take risks and venture out of my comfort zone.

I think back to my first exchange trip to Germany in 1967.

Mixing Cultures

I suppose it was hearing so much Yiddish in my childhood that made it easy for me to learn German. I certainly didn't ever struggle with the language and the patterns and sounds always felt incredibly familiar. Mum didn't discourage me from wanting to go to Germany when the opportunity for an exchange came up, but she was justifiably a little anxious that I should not be put with a family that was anti-Semitic. She had been badly treated when she was evacuated during the war years because she was Jewish, which prematurely forced her back to London.

My teachers promised to find me a suitable placement with a family who was aware of my ethnic background. Things were all set to go ahead. A few days before I was due to leave, the family that had agreed to take me pulled out. Miss Butler, the Deputy Head, came into my classroom wielding a letter. Another family had stepped in at the last minute. "They have a girl, Sabine, your age, and a son, Peter two years younger. There are no photos and no time to send any. Will you still go?"

As I was supposed to be leaving that weekend it was a snap decision. Mum and Dad agreed I should make the trip so a few days later I was on the twenty-six hour sailing from Harwich to Hamburg on the Prinz Hamlet ferry. I was sixteen years-old, and though used to travelling on my own, I was apprehensive about the mystery family and how I would settle in.

In Hamburg I boarded a train bound for Lübeck. The Zahns had arranged to meet me there. With no photos for ID it was bound to be an interesting rendezvous.

Days later, Bine (as Sabine liked to be called) told me what happened at the station: "We had no idea what to expect. We scrutinised all the passengers as they got off the train. Then we saw this enormous bandy-legged grotesque looking girl with braces on her teeth, wiry hair and a lopsided grin. She looked very vacant and for many horrible moments we thought we were lumbered. I tried to hide round the corner, but my Mum insisted we go to greet her. We started walking towards her, but she ignored us and went straight past. Then we saw you waving! What a relief!"

Bine was slim, with long blond hair, blue eyes and roughly hewn Nordic features.

I felt really at home with the Zahns. Bine and Peter both shared my sense of humour. Peter reminded me of Gerald in the way that he constantly teased his sister and his father. It all felt very normal. There were few cultural exchanges between families in those days and some barriers to break down. The Zahns were concerned that as an English girl I would only eat beefsteak. I explained that I wasn't fussy and enjoyed most things with the exception of beetroot. It was great for me to sample German filter coffee served with thick evaporated milk and to sleep under a feather bed (duvet) for the first time ever.

Bine's Father, Fritz Zahn, had a kind, slightly wizened face, as though he had spent far more than his sixty-six years on the planet. He was proud to tell me that he'd built the house himself after the war. He also showed me the diaries that he had kept during the whole conflict. He would have been arrested had they been found since they were full of anti-Hitler comments. He and many of his fellow Wehrmacht soldiers quickly realised that Germany was not heading for victory but for disaster.

Fritz was bursting with little aphorisms, always spoke slowly and clearly in a voice I could understand. Under his patient tutoring my grasp of German improved dramatically.

Fritz was so much older than his son that they found each other difficult to tolerate; another familiar scenario for me!

The Zahns had no bathroom yet, but a small shower unit in the basement, and a sink for every day use in the parental bedroom. On the first morning Bine told me I could go through the bedroom and use the sink. I was a little embarrassed since I saw what I thought were Herr and Frau Zahn still in bed. I waited for ages, but there was no movement. Eventually, hearing their voices downstairs, I realised that the lumps I had mistaken for Bine's parents were just the bulky featherbeds still in situ.

Fritz Zahn rose early every weekday morning to run his garage business in Hamburg. In his absence Ilse, his wife, looked after me well.

On my return to the UK, I introduced my family to German coffee, Quark (like Fromage Frais), and more importantly the Duvet.

A few months later Bine came over to our house to practise her halting English, which wasn't helped by Gerald's efforts to confuse her as much as possible. He managed to convince her that mustard was custard, and taunted her with endless tins of baked beans, thrusting them under her chin: "This is you Beeeeeena!"

Fortunately it didn't stop her trips to Ardwell Avenue, since she could see the funny side of Gerald. We laughed over her quaint phrases.

She told us very earnestly about a half sister who lived in London: "My sister is short-eyed. She wears her hair upstairs. Her parting is sometimes on the left side, sometimes on the backside." Then Bine asked me if I knew a song by Elvis Presley, *Let the Hard Eggs Begin*. She wanted to know exactly what it was about. It was difficult to stop laughing long enough to explain!

My initial trip was the first of many exchanges between our families.

In 1969 I took Bine to see the Rolling Stones in Hyde Park. The music was stunning, and the atmosphere at this free concert unique. Coming from a small city like Lübeck, Bine had never experienced such a large-scale event. She was thrilled and climbed over endless people to get to the front with her camera. I still have those self-developed black and white photographs of Jagger, Richards, Wyman, Watts and Brian Jones' replacement, Mick Taylor, that Bine risked life and limb to take. They capture not just the excitement of the day, but of the whole Sixties era.

The Stones in the Park (1969)

One Christmas Bine and Peter taught me to ice skate. They literally took one arm each pulled me for the first four kilometres along the frozen Wagnitz river, and I tentatively managed the second four kilometres myself. It was brilliant.

My Mum and Dad made the trip to visit Ilse long after Fritz Zahn died, and they found similar hospitality on their arrival. In taking a risk by staying with a completely unknown family I made a lifelong friend.

Bine and I are still in regular touch with each other. She has just finished a course of chemo for breast cancer. We plan to meet again just as soon as we are able.

Diary – 1st November 2007

The 'Freighter Blight' has really taken hold to the point where I have to get checked out at the hospital to see if they can give me some cream for the rash. I feel tired today at the least exertion, so do very little in the way of activities.

It was Halloween last night and I wasn't in the mood to open the door to trick-or-treaters, so I ignored them in curmudgeonly fashion. I could probably have gone trick or treating without any disguise but I didn't want to scare the neighbours.

Minna sees me at the hospital to look at my skin. The bubble is burst. She is not connected with Count Dracula at all, but is from Finland.

After examining my unsightly rash, Dr B and his registrar decide between them what lotion to prescribe. I ask about the next batch of scans due around January. I don't want to wait three weeks for them!

"Oh yes," says Dr B. "You will have to keep bringing that to our attention." It is so difficult to have confidence in a team that is so disorganised and has such little communication between colleagues.

I take the prescription to pharmacy, where they make an art form of keeping folks waiting with a system of tickets and extended periods of ceiling watching. I am told it will be at least half an hour before I receive the medication, yet there are only two people in front of me. I have now spent an hour at St Mary's and it is an hour too long. I think hospitals are designed to be frustrating. As I watch the impatient faces around me a man on crutches asks the way to the fracture clinic. I envy him. Two months or so in plaster and he will probably make a full recovery.

On my way home I pop into the supermarket. The checkout girl is chatty: "And how are you today?"

Despite her apparent enthusiasm I know I can't answer truthfully or the poor lass would wish she'd never asked. Then she launches into grade one monologue mode. I find out how tired she is (mate's eighteenth birthday party 'til late) and all about which programmes won the national awards last night on TV at the Royal Albert Hall. I am bombarded with information on soaps, which I've never seen. I try to smile and nod in the right places despite urgently wanting her to be quiet.

In the end I tell her I saw Coronation Street when it was in black and white. I feel old.

Jobs through the decades

In the Sixties and Seventies I had a succession of casual jobs. Whilst still at school I was helping my aunt in her hairdresser's for about a year before I finally landed a 'proper' Saturday job in Woolworth's at Stratford Broadway. It was very different from the stores we see today. Goods were displayed on separate counters, each with its own cash register and serving staff.

Of course we, the sixteen year-old 'Saturday girls', as they called us, were the most menial in the hierarchy. We were given a counter to supervise for the day. That meant walking up and down (we weren't allowed to sit for the full eight hour shift). If there were no customers, we were expected to clean the glass frames, and look busy. The cash tills were large and noisy, and needed a fair bit of strength to hold down the keys and push back the drawer. We had to count the change carefully. Any discrepancies would be docked from our twenty-five shilling wages. Twenty-five shillings was equivalent to one pound twenty-five, though the buying power would probably be between ten and fifteen pounds today.

My favourite counter was jewellery, as we got to repair broken items and it was never that busy. The worst was the Christmas card counter! There wasn't time to think and we were taking money all day. It was very tiring. The breaks were welcome, but short. We were scorned by the permanent staff, who treated us like scum, and patronised us. They had reached the pinnacle of their careers as sales assistants and were jealous that we had higher aspirations.

The most intimidating member of staff was our Under Manager Mr Jeffries, who carried himself with authority and whose face showed his distain for us mere mortals. Mr Jeffries was always in control. He spoke in a dark mellow voice, which rarely varied in intonation. He held himself erect at all times, with his eyelids slightly closed, as though he wanted to minimise visual contact with the rest of humanity. With the irreverence of youth we nicknamed him 'God'. He was so tall that he had to stoop to hear customer's requests. In those days most transactions were cash. Any time that a customer wrote a cheque, we had to summon Mr Jeffries.

On one occasion, a man staggered over to me, shouting and complaining and waving a suitcase in the air. I could smell the alcohol on his breath. He made a lot of fuss and demanded to see the manager. He wanted to return the suitcase that he had purchased the previous week. I rang my bell and waited, nervous as I watched an impatient queue gathering at my counter. It was a relief to see the Under Manager's measured steps as he approached the noisy red-faced customer. There was an exchange of words. The Under Manager then strode purposefully over to me, bent down, and with his voice unchanged from his usual monotone he whispered quietly into my ear: "Give this bloody nuisance his money back."

This was customer service 1960s style.

In contrast, my job at the London Hospital Whitechapel in the early Seventies in my University holidays was much less pressured. I was employed as an orderly there, mostly working in the nurses homes; cleaning, general dogsbody, anything they could find for me. Being a conscientious sort of person, I would turn my hand to anything, without any fuss. One day, most of the chores completed, my line manager asked me if I would take a stiff brush and help the regular orderlies scrub a row of armchairs in the nurses' lounge. I set to work as requested. After about half an hour I noticed that my co-workers had mysteriously disappeared. When I ran out of detergent a few minutes later I realised what was going on. Three of them were huddled in the stock cupboard furtively smoking. They looked up guiltily when I opened the door, and were clearly relieved to see it was me. Then they initiated me into the conspiracy. The advice was simple: "We spend all day doing as little as possible! This is a great hiding place. They never bother looking in here."

The energy it took to do this earned my undying admiration. I declined the invitation to join them, and we happily agreed to differ.

Work at the hospital was on a rota. The most interesting shift was from 1pm until 9.30. In the evenings after 8pm we got to do reception duty in the nurses' home, which was quite cosy really; simple tasks of drawing the curtains on the main floor, and delivering the milk to each of the annexes. It would arrive thick white and foamy in large copper urns, from which we would ladle it into smaller vessels. It was a satisfying task. When all the chores were complete we would sit huddled at the concierge's desk, giving out the occasional key to late arrivals and sipping hot chocolate made from the fresh milk we had just distributed. I don't remember anyone getting sick from that milk, but I'm sure it would send a frisson of horror into a modern food hygiene inspector. I personally didn't ever see creepy crawlies in the milk, but more than likely they would have sunk plump satiated and happy to the bottom of the urn.

Venturing home at that time of night on the tube from Whitechapel to Hainault was always a challenge. Many a time there would be weirdoes lurking in the underground in various states of inebriation. One evening I was part shocked and part fascinated to see a man carted off in a straight-jacket at Mile End station.

In 1972 I spent a year in Erlangen, West Germany, as part of my University studies. Instead of returning home for the Easter break, I applied for a job as a copy typist with Siemens for a month. It was difficult to work out why they even took me on. I was hardly one of their most efficient employees. My typing speed was dismally slow,

I had never used an electric typewriter in my life, the German keyboard is set out differently and I was still just a student of the language.

The office staff appeared to be incredibly tolerant of my numerous clerical disasters and my poor output. They seemed to enjoy my company and were very friendly. No work could start until the morning ritual of hand shaking was over. Each member of the office staff had to both give and receive greetings. This was very time consuming since it was a very formalised ceremony.

"Guten Morgen Frau Schmidt/Fraulein Zimmer/Herr Braun."

As soon as 11am came along it was customary to wish any new entrant to the room 'Mahlzeit'. This is how Germans herald all their meals, but lunch was not for another two hours.

As well as hearty handshaking, everyone in the office obeyed the clock. We worked from 7.30 in the morning until 4.30pm. At precisely 4.25pm every day the staff would down tools and clear their desks to sit and watch the big hand move round to the half hour. No one would dream of leaving a second earlier, even though not a stroke of work was done in that last five minutes. Then would come a lengthy round of "Auf wiedersehen Frau Schmidt/Fraulein Zimmer/Herr Braun," plus the customary handshaking.

When I think of how hard the workforce is driven by managers nowadays in so many different fields of employment it really was much more relaxed in the Seventies.

Of course we didn't have the strict adherence to equal opportunities that exists nowadays. When I attended my very first interview for a teaching post in a posh suburban school in 1974, there was very little feedback from the Headmaster as to why he preferred the male applicant to me. His explanation was quite simply this: "My sixth form boys might fall in love with you."

For my second interview I set my sights lower. I applied for a post in a tough North West London Comprehensive. I should have been suspicious when I was the only candidate at interview. The school was high up on the 'Social Priorities' list. A member of staff had been stabbed there the previous year. It wasn't difficult to fulfil the Headmaster's criteria, which seemed to consist of willingness to work in a multi cultural environment, the ability to stand up for forty minutes at a time, and the absence of a severe nervous tick.

The most challenging question he asked me was: "If we offered you the post, would you take it?"

How times have changed.

Needless to say they did offer me the job and I survived there for two years, leaving long before the nervous tick became obvious!

But that's another story…

Diary – 2nd November 2007

Another weekly dose of the trial drug (Cetuximab) in the Chemotherapy Suite today. Anita, my escort from the Wessex Cancer Trust, is proving to be a reliable and interesting companion. She and I solve the world's problems on the way into Newport. I'm not sure anyone notices. I have my watch back at last, after leaving it on the bedside table last time. Having it back seems more important to me right now.

Today there are difficulties with the canula like last week. The first insertion causes extreme inflammation and has to be removed. It sets the process back by an hour. Next Thursday I go for the pre-chemo blood test and check-up with Dr B.

Friday's treatment will be the second of eight all day sessions. I have a week free of tablets ahead and intend to make the most of it!

5th November

My mouth and hands are sore and I feel nauseous despite being off the tablets this week. I hear on the news this morning that there is widespread fog on the Mainland. I think back to the infamous smogs of my childhood. I could do with one right now to conceal my face from the general public. My skin continues to erupt into unsightly spots lumps and red marks.

It is becoming depressing even to look in the mirror.

The Pea-Souper

London became famous for its smogs. Tourists visited the capital just to see it, and could even buy souvenir tins of 'London fog'. But the fumes brought health problems – lung and eye irritations, agues, rheumatism and fevers.

By the early twentieth century the declining use of coal, along with tighter industrial controls, saw a reduction in smog, but 'air quality was still sufficiently poor for the infamous London smog of 1952, which lasted five days, was to cause 4,000 deaths.' (Patrick Barkham, *The Times*, 8th August 2003)

As a child I would often see buses travelling at crawling speed, with volunteers holding lanterns or torches in front of them to light their way. Old people and small babies had to be kept at home, because their lungs couldn't breathe in the air very safely.

To get to school I walk from Deanery Road, along Water Lane and then up to the Point. My large classroom has small wooden desks. Each desk has its own inkwell. Behind the teacher's desk stands the large blackboard, which has thin lines, embossed upon it for demonstrating handwriting. An open fire surrounded by a large mesh fireguard nestles in the corner of the room. When my teacher has a cold she tosses her used tissues into the fire and I love to watch them curl and shrivel, as they are slowly devoured by the bold yellow flames. The acrid smell lingers unpleasantly. From time to time, particularly in November, we have thick fogs known as 'pea-soupers'.

One November afternoon in 1958 when I am seven years-old, we are surprised when Mrs Nobbs says that we all have to go to the assembly hall. It is now so foggy that when we look out of the windows the playground has disappeared and we can't see the school gates. The Headmaster's voice sounds serious.

"School will close this afternoon. There is a dangerous pea-souper. No-one is allowed to go home until they are collected."

I feel excited at the prospect of disappearing into the depths of the murk. What an adventure!

Parents begin arriving one by one to pick up their children. After about ten minutes I see Mum. She is wearing a thick, hairy, dark green coat. I am looking forward to walking home with her.

"Now I want you to be a good girl," she says. "Put this scarf round your face and hold my hand tightly. You have to keep the scarf on so that you don't breathe in the fumes."

We step out into an eerie silent world of swirling yellow mist. It is so thick that the smoky bitterness coats my tongue. We start walking slowly towards Water Lane.

"We'll have to be really careful crossing the main road." Mum's voice is strangely muffled behind her scarf. "Now put one foot in front of the other, but be careful of the kerb."

I look down. "But Mummy I can't see my feet!" I exclaim.

We tread gingerly down the kerb into the road and try to cross in a straight line. We have no way of knowing where the road finishes, or even if we are still walking in the right direction.

"Now hold my arm, and we will take really tiny steps… try to feel the kerb with your feet so you don't trip." Mum's voice is reassuring as ever and I have every confidence that we will be safe. It's exhilarating to cover familiar terrain but to experience it so differently using senses beyond sight.

We shuffle along like this for what seems like an age. We cross a road, but struggle to find the other side, losing our sense of direction completely.

"Ouch! What's that…?"

We have bumped into a lamp-post, but didn't see it.

"Look, Mummy. We're home." I peer at the road sign and trace the large embossed black letters with my finger. "Deanery Road."

Mum chuckles. "Now we just need to find the house!"

It is both weird and thrilling being out in that fog, knowing we are so close to our house, but not being able to see it.

Diary – 9th November 2007

Chris tells me I should visualise myself as a chrysalis. I am undergoing a metamorphosis. The skin rash, the nausea, is all part of the process. When the treatment is finished I will materialise transformed. I think it is a lovely analogy and I hope he is right. I feel more like the human host in Alien. What will emerge?

Had my bloods taken yesterday at the hospital. Dr. B says they were fine so the next lot of chemo can go ahead as planned tomorrow. He tells me they have found six liver tumours not five, but that the sixth should be operable. He is prescribing some vitamin B6 for the soreness in my fingertips.

I ask Chris if he thinks the treatments will vary during the holiday period. Chris thinks they will probably add Christmas Pudding to the infusion. That wasn't exactly what I had in mind.

When I arrive for chemo today Minna tells me they have the CEA result, which is the cancer 'marker'. It has gone down from 911.7 to 381.3 – which shows something is working. My relief is palpable.

They use a larger needle in my vein to reduce the pain of the Oxaliplatin. Feels like a bayonet to me. Most of the day I am okay but just when I am due to come home I feel suddenly really sick and Anita, who is waiting for me, calls the nurse. I vomit a few times and feel wretched. They don't understand why I have been affected like this. The first anti-emetic doesn't work too well and I have to wait another half an hour. Then they realise that one of the nurses forgot to give me the anti-sickness medication with the Oxaliplatin, so they try me with tablets. I bring them straight back up. At the same time my arm pumps blood profusely all over the floor where they took out the needle. The nurses are running around with bowls and swabs like the Keystone Cops. The floor looks like the aftermath of an Inspector Morse murder.

An hour later they finally let me out after yet another injection this *time in my left arm. Anita has been waiting patiently to drive me home. She is a saint. She brings several sick bowls and wipes from the hospital and tells me not to worry if I throw up in the car. Luckily I don't.*

Not a great day. A couple of hours later I manage one slice of dry toast and go to bed.

I have a bad night, feeling sick on and off. This morning I can't even put my socks on because my fingers are so prickly and painful. I burst into tears and feel sorry for myself. I have some breakfast of toast and pills, but the change of temperature from bed triggers such severe neuropathy that I shelve my plans to go for a walk and decide to stay in bed instead.

It is not like me to give in like this. I have crossed a border this year from health into sickness. I am not enjoying the trip.

East Berlin

During my student year in Erlangen we went on a week's organised tour to Berlin. This involved a coach trip into East Germany, and then on to West Berlin. We were held up for two hours at the border into West Berlin whilst the East German guards made a thorough search of the coach inside and out using mirrors to check that there were no escapees hiding under the seats.

Our day trip to East Berlin was a dramatic contrast to the affluent West, where shop frontages boasted an extravaganza of fur coats, calf-skin knee-high boots and high fashion garments with price tags that we impoverished students could only marvel at.

Entering East Berlin through Check Point Charlie was like stepping back in time. This was 1972 but there was no more than a scattering of two-stroke smoky Trabbis (Trabant cars) on the road. In the shops there were no advertisements for products, just signs on the windows telling shoppers what was in stock. People didn't make lists. They bought what was available.

There were communist slogans everywhere: *Arbeit macht frei* (Work Liberates) with the familiar hammer and sickle. No one seemed particularly keen to serve us, and people's eyes looked dull with disinterest. In a café where we went for lunch they plonked bowls of soup in front of us that looked muddy and tasted of watery cabbage. I could empathise with George Orwell's Winston Smith, in *1984*, attempting to eat his spongy pink meat substitute.

In one shop we encountered a stooped old woman in a shabby grey coat who was keen to show us her tin of meat.

"I bought this for tomorrow. It's a religious holiday see. But *they* don't acknowledge it, that lot." She waved her finger vaguely in the air. "I'm going to stay in and celebrate all by myself." She was having her own private rebellion against the State and had shared her little secret with us. We felt privileged.

Browsing through a local bookshop I was astounded at the poor quality of the rough yellowing paper in each book. I was fascinated by *English for You (Book 7)* – a schoolbook for students. Most of the text was strike- or unemployment-related propaganda: translate, "I was going to join the protesters. Thousands of British workers demonstrated their unanimous will to fight the anti-union laws by strikes and mass demonstrations in 1971."

According to the textbook British families were poor, most workers were on strike, pay was bad and the fathers in the family were all reading the *Daily Star*. Intrigued, I bought a copy.

Some of my friends bought cigarettes and couldn't believe that the tobacco was packed so loosely that it fell out as they lit up. The chocolate tasted like ash. The supermarkets were lined with hundreds of jars of beetroot and jam, and brand choices were restricted to Polish or Russian.

Berlin was completely separated. It was possible for Westerners to pass from one to the other only through strictly-controlled checkpoints. For most Easterners, travel to West Berlin or West Germany was no longer possible. In 1971, a Four-Power agreement guaranteed access across East Germany to West Berlin and ended the potential for harassment or closure of the routes.

I came away with mixed feelings. Part of me felt ashamed to return to the affluent Kurfürstendam in West Berlin, part of me was relieved to be living in a free country.

Diary – 11th November 2007

I feel so awful on Sunday that I fall into bed at 5.30pm, nauseous and exhausted. An hour later I wake to eat a piece of toast and to take the dreaded chemo pills which can only be swallowed after food. I then sleep on.

My dreams are really vivid. Vignettes of work play over in my mind. In each scene I am unable to do the job properly; they have changed the keyboard so I can't log onto my computer. I feel remote from what is going on, and can't keep up with it all. Then I see my Mum with her soft brown laughing eyes and her head of thick chestnut hair. We have a cuddle and I feel a bond of love so strong it makes me feel warm secure and loved. I think back to those happy times in her company.

Holiday in the sun, 1966

Miles of white sandy beaches, cries of 'Gelati Mocha' from colourfully dressed ice-cream sellers, blue skies and limitless sunshine…

These are not the most vivid memories that linger when I think back to our family holiday in Catolica, in 1966. What stays with me is my Mum's infectious laugh and the fun I had, aged fifteen, and being abroad for the first time.

Our family had once ventured to France on a day trip when I was five years-old, so Italy was an exotic prospect. Previous family vacations had been at Margate in the sort of B&Bs with puritanical landladies who monitored the number of grains of sand you brought in to the boarding house, and who were tight-lipped with disapproval if you attempted to carry a bucket and spade upstairs. They were rigidly strict about what time you came home in the evening, making every effort to dampen any holiday spirit that might survive their inhospitable regime.

The freedom of the modern hotel seemed, to the four of us, like the dizzy heights of luxury. Mum, Dad and my brother Gerald spoke not a word of Italian. Given that I did French and German at school they were dependant on my linguistic skills. Desperate not to let them down I had eagerly memorised some phrases in preparation so I was embarrassed when on the first morning at breakfast, Dad spat out his first mouthful of tea.

"That is disgusting!" he gasped.

Disbelieving, we each had a taste, but had to agree. It was quite undrinkable and all my fault; I had made the classic error of mixing up *caldo* with *fredo* – and hot milk in tea is a noxious potion. My family did not allow me to forget it for the remainder of the two weeks and for some considerable time afterwards.

We had high expectations the first night we gathered in the vast dining room, expecting a meal to match the décor; colourful and impressive. Sadly, the pasta with tomato sauce, the soup of unknown origin, the meat dish and the dessert peach, everything was red with an orange hue. Every mouthful smelled and tasted the same.

By the third night we were loosing hope that the repetitious diet might vary. Thus my Dad's words to Mum, uttered every night for two weeks, became immortalised in our family archives: "What's the matter, Frances? You used to like a peach once!"

In an attempt to stimulate our palates with the addition of jam at breakfast, Mum and I went on a shopping trip in the local resort. We ventured into a small grocer's shop, which smelt of an interesting mix of goat's cheese and olives. My phrase book didn't do jam. Though the elderly shopkeeper was very friendly, in response to our inadequate miming he climbed his creaky wooden ladder, eagerly depositing tinned soups, tomato sauce, various jars of pickled delicacies onto the counter before us. But alas, no jam.

I shook my head. He looked mortified. When he had arrayed most of his stock for our perusal, I thought I would try my French on him, so I asked for 'la confiture'.

His wrinkled face lit up with delight, and with a beaming smile he suddenly grabbed me and started waltzing round the shop crying out intermittently in his beautifully lilting Italian: "Ahhh! La confitura, la marmalada!" He was almost in tears with relief. He kept shaking our hands and dancing with joy.

After our purchase there were many more minutes of hand shaking before Mum and I escaped his clutches.

We were still giggling when we went into a local bar half an hour later to sample some cappuccinos. In the dark smoky room Mum caught sight of a mechanised table football game. Unable to resist, she challenged me to a match. We had no chance of understanding the instructions, but it looked straightforward: two teams, red and blue, with the footballers on fixed track runners. We thought it would be relatively easy. We couldn't have been more misguided!

Mum stood at one end and I stood at the other, perched in expectation, fingers on buttons. In went the *Lire*, but instead of the ordered game we were expecting, the machine suddenly started shaking, emitting a high-pitched whining noise. It spat out tiny white balls at intervals, and – quite without warning – the figures began spurting up and down the pitch, sporadically making contact with the ball. Despite our best efforts, we couldn't work out which of us was operating which players.

"Are you the blues then?" I asked, as I frantically tried to control the reds.

"I haven't a clue! Who's winning?" came Mum's feverish response as she tried to make some impact on the action.

Nothing we did made a jot of difference. We soon abandoned the controls and just watched in amazement. One look at Mum's face, eyes wide, mouth agape and looking completely baffled, set me off laughing. Mum joined in, her eyes fixed on the scene below the glass screen of the football table where the players were manically propelling themselves from one end of the pitch to the other. Our laughter intensified and began to attracted attention from some of the locals, who paused from their beers and coffees to stare at us as though we had totally lost our minds.

The incongruity of the situation exacerbated our already hysterical laughter. The more we tried to control ourselves, in front of our bemused audience, the less capable we became of being coherent. We laughed until our sides ached, we could hardly stand upright. By now we were clinging helplessly to the table, tears rolling down our faces watching the frenzied red and blue figures.

It was only when the money ran out that the whirring abated and the players gradually lost momentum, coming eventually to a complete stop. Then heads turned towards the two slightly hysterical, wobbly and seemingly crazy English women as they crept sheepishly away from that bar and stepped outside, arm in arm, into the reality of the warm Catolica sunshine. Ah, moments to treasure forever.

Diary – 12th November 2007

I am having a bad week. The nausea is with me most of the time and I can eat very little. Water tastes like cream; disgusting, but I am so thirsty. I spend the first couple of hours of the day in bed.

Simone from the chemo unit rings me to see how I am. She suggests I visit the GP for another anti-sickness drug – Cyclizine. I make an appointment for 3.30pm, but Dr P emerges from his room after ten minutes as he has been called out on an emergency. I wait nearly an hour for him to return, by which time I am feeling even more nauseous. He apologises for keeping me waiting and saying very little beyond that, he writes a prescription for the suggested drug.

I wander home across the green, feeling too ill to go to the chemist. Chris is exhausted when he gets home and all the neighbours are out, so it has to wait until tomorrow.

It still amazes me that tears come to me fairly easily nowadays. As a child I grew up to believe they were a sign of weakness. Being called 'waterworks' or 'cry-baby' by my Dad and Gerald on a regular basis served only to reinforce such feelings. I learnt very quickly how to suppress tears and deny vulnerability, coating myself with a tough outer shell that was frequently mistaken for coldness and lack of empathy. My outer crust still leads people to believe that I am strong, but those closest to me know my soft centre: small, anxious and afraid.

The counselling course I embarked on in the mid-Nineties helped me to uncover some blind spots, and I gradually came to realise that it was unhealthy to cover up ones inner feelings all the time, and that everyone needs a few trusted people, friends and family, to open up to. This has also helped my empathy with others and I can see that such emotions are reciprocal.

This morning I prepare a couple of hand warming gel pads and cycle the couple of miles to the chemist for the prescription. The warmth makes the neuropathy tolerable. On my return, still feeling sick and desperate to drink something that tastes nice, I just burst into tears. I sit on the stairs sobbing for about five minutes, feeling really sorry for myself. I discover that fresh grapefruit squeezed into hot water tastes fine, so I make a large mug of that which makes me feel a little better.

Kate from the chemo unit calls and has some sensible suggestions as to what I might try. She tells me I should ring them tomorrow morning if I am still having problems.

When I see Simone at the Chemotherapy Suite, she tells me she had to buy a new pair of shoes following last Friday's debacle. It wasn't until Anita pointed out the trail of blood she was walking across the floor that she realised I had bled profusely into the old pair! I am not sure whether to laugh or feel bad. I laugh.

The doctor prescribes another anti-emetic. It is called Domperidone. To me it sounds more like champagne. Imagine my disappointment when I discover it tastes nothing like it.

The week becomes better, though I am still limited outdoors because of the continuing neuropathy and the colder weather.

I bury myself in a book and escape.

Escape

I am curled up on my bed in Deanery Road, Valour heater glowing gently in the corner taking the sting of winter from the air. I am so absorbed by *Five go to Kirrin Island* that most of Sunday passes in a haze. I am a passionate reader.

Mum had derived huge amounts of enjoyment from books and wanted me to share her pleasure. Since there were no computers and little on TV beyond *Andy Pandy*, *Muffin the Mule* and *Bill and Ben*, reading was the one escapist pastime that really worked for me. When I first learned to read Mum took me to the children's library and helped me choose. I remember picking up a book entitled, *The Reluctant Dragon*.

My curiosity aroused I asked, "Mummy what does 'reluctant' mean?"

"It means 'unwilling'."

In this way my vocabulary soon expanded and I became an avid and confident reader. From those early days of reading the HP sauce bottle with Grandpa, I went on a journey into books with numerous childhood favourites.

When I wanted to get away from real life, I was enveloped by the new worlds within those printed pages. The words took me to exciting places where I discovered hidden treasures. By reading, generally all day on a Sunday, my imagination was fuelled. From early children's stories I progressed to Enid Blyton's *Famous Five*. I was on Kirrin Island with George, Dick, Julian, Anne and Timmy. Georgina was a Tomboy just like me, and I so admired her short hairstyle and headstrong nature. She wasn't girlie, and nor was I. I longed for a dog as clever as Timmy. I shared lives with them all. Julian appeared to be twelve going on eighteen and Anne was ten going on thirty! They hardly ever had contact with their parents, since they were always together during the holidays, and at different boarding schools in term time. It was a children's world. Grown-ups didn't belong, except as a backdrop to provide the baddies against whom the children pitted their wits. I was there with them in the depths of secret passages or on the moors in howling gales. I feasted on their delicious sandwiches and sausage rolls washed down with copious swigs of ginger beer, smelling and tasting the food as it passed their lips. This was my virtual world.

I was so excited when the Five caught smugglers, or cracked a secret code. Mum would sometimes pound on my door just as one of the Five was about to be captured by the pirates.

"Are you coming downstairs? You've been up here for hours."

"In a minute", I would mumble and, trance unbroken, I was instantly back in the smuggler's caves eager to read on.

It didn't matter one jot that the books encouraged sexist attitudes. I read them at face value. I did not see their flaws.

When I had satiated my appetite for those Kirrin adventures and had digested each of the twenty-one stories Enid Blyton wrote, I moved on.

I found a deep affinity with my childhood heroines. In Coolidge's *What Katy Did* I admired Katy's transformation of character. Having been confined to bed after a nasty accident where she damages her back she is frequently sour and moody, snapping at her family who are trying to do their best for her. Despite phenomenal boredom to be imprisoned in bed at such a young age, Katy gradually learns compassion, selflessness and the ability to help those around her feel good about themselves. She is a role model I would love to emulate today. Having undergone more than a month in hospital myself and with an enforced long period of sickness I can see what a hard lesson it is to learn, and that it comes only after a struggle.

I wept for Spyri's *Heidi* too; a young girl who values the simple things in life, and who thrives in the open air, becoming ill when forced to live in the large city of Frankfurt. She shows remarkable strength of character, is kind and gentle to her blind Grandmother, and her childish innocence has always influenced me. Back then I saw her free spirit within myself and feel similarly today. Trapped in a city I feel like a caged tiger. When countryside and the sea surround me, I feel I am at home and that these are my roots. Heidi felt the same way. We both pine for the fresh air, the outdoors and freedom.

Another childhood favourite (which I read as a young teenager) was AJ Cronin's *Hatter's Castle*, where the heroine has to cope with huge adversity. Mary is forced from her home run by her tyrannical Scottish father, and has to leave because she is pregnant. Her journey through that stormy night in pain and discomfort always represents for me a metaphor of life. We face our demons, and if we have strength and courage like Mary, we get through.

Being a passionate reader turned me into a bit of an isolate. I was content to read and explore my imagination, rather than face the real world. Mum was quite worried about me at times. She felt that I didn't socialise enough and would encourage me to go out with friends when they rang. I would often decline, preferring to spend my time with my favourite fictional characters. I hated discos and dances; I always felt like I was 'on display' waiting for boys to ask me to dance. When I did get dances, I couldn't even hold a conversation since the music was so loud. I just found it all incredibly boring. What I did enjoy was going swimming with the club or on organised rambles.

Such hermit-like tendencies are still with me. When I go out, I want to engage in activities that interest me. I like my own company and need sufficient 'alone time' to regenerate. Though I have long outgrown *The Famous Five*, I still love to loose myself within the pages of a good book.

Diary – 24th November 2007

I finally rang County Hall yesterday to find out what happens with my pay. I will be on half pay from January, so I need to claim incapacity benefit. I have been putting this off, as the thought of filling in more forms is a daunting prospect. Still, the deed is done, and hopefully my brain will be able to absorb the contents of the booklet that will help me understand exactly what I am supposed to do.

This should be a good week. I am free of tablets and have to regain some strength ready for next Friday's drug bombardment. Yesterday went really smoothly – they inserted the drip after only one failed attempt and I was away by midday.

I am feeling so much better this week. There is very little residual nausea and it is wonderful to be able to enjoy food. I am finding that I crave good homemade soup. It is easy to digest and simple to prepare. In response to a resurrection of my appetite I have a 'soupfest' this week making different varieties on alternate days. I begin with basil and tomato, move on to leek and lentil, progress from there to fresh pea soup followed by mushroom and the finale – a delicious cauliflower and ginger.

Everyone I speak to on the telephone remarks on my bravery. Though it is encouraging to be viewed in this way, I don't personally see my attitude as courageous. I have to keep going. The alternative is unthinkable.

27th November

A surprise telephone call from the Medical Centre this morning. Dr C wants to come round to see me, to find out how things are going. That's a first!

Dr C turns up within ten minutes of the call. I think he is as shocked at the diagnosis as I am. He had been to see me initially when I was taken ill and had not expected this outcome. He is very understanding and tells me I should call into the surgery if there are any problems. He agrees that I shouldn't be going into work because of the risks of infection; that could set me back weeks in the treatment.

It's embarrassing when I take him into the lounge; the new suite hasn't arrived yet and we are using garden chairs indoors. It reminds me of the time when Daniel was a few months old; the health visitor came round to our house in Maidenhead but we had no furniture and were living out of suitcases. We had recently returned from South Africa and all our stuff was still at the depot because of a lorry driver's strike. I was explaining the situation to her when she suddenly looked around the room and announced: "I remember this place." She had been our tenant while we were abroad!

When I see Dr B again, he is really pleased with my progress. He believes the pain I was experiencing a few weeks ago was caused by pressure from one of the tumours. He examines me and is reasonably confident that the tumours are beginning to shrink. He tells me that the liver surgeons will operate as long as the awkward tumour does not increase in size, which is now highly unlikely. He is chasing up the scans with Southampton to pre-empt any possible delays. My blood test was fine, so chemotherapy goes ahead tomorrow.

I am relieved that things appear to be going smoothly. There are now only two more chemo sessions before the operation. Then I will have come half way. A milestone indeed.

I am reading a book on paranormal experiences whilst on chemo, and I think back to the time when Mum was in the Hospice.

Sixth Sense

I rarely experience intuitive flashes but one that really sticks in my mind is when Mum was dying.

Every one knew she couldn't last more than a few hours. They had stopped feeding her the week before and the nurses had prepared Dad for the inevitable. It struck me she was hanging on until he could 'allow' her to die and could come to terms with it.

I sat with her day and night. As I watched her I had a sudden incredibly clear vision of a clock above the bed saying one o'clock. In that moment I knew she would die at that time.

I told Gerald about my vision. It was early evening and Gerald said he would go home and I was to call him when it was all over. I was fine with that. I understood why he couldn't be there at the moment of death.

The night passed uneventfully, and I assumed my premonition had been wrong. Just before one o'clock the following afternoon, Dad went to get a cup of tea… and I am certain Mum waited until he left before she let go. A few minutes later as I sat with her she took her last breath. It was just after one pm. I had been right all along. I was devastated losing her, but had been praying for merciful release. It was unbearable to watch her suffer and knowing she was now at peace was a huge relief.

Rachel too had that gift of premonition, though the case she related to me was infinitely less significant. She told me that for some time she had avoided touching a door at school, not really understanding why until she saw the large WET PAINT notice on that door just a few days later.

When Rachel was just over two years-old I had a conversation with her about when I was pregnant. She asked where she was when Daniel was born.

"Was I a tiny baby?"

"Yes. Where were you?"

"I was still in the river."

I just thought it was childish prattle and didn't see any significance, but subsequently I have read about possibilities of pre-birth memories and years later I replayed the tape and nearly fell off my chair. Rachel clearly had a distinct memory of being in a river before she was born. It still amazes me to this day.

I think there is more to life than we sometimes realise.

Diary – 30th November 2007

Good news again today. The cancer marker in yesterday's blood test is down again by more than half to just over a hundred.

The statistics so far:

Date	Marker
11.10.07	*911.7*
08.11.07	*381.3*
29.11.07	*102.7*

I hope the trend continues!

Minna asks me if I will help with more research. It involves another blood test and questionnaire. I don't hesitate. If I can contribute to a cure then I am happy to help. She explains the next expectation in research, which is to develop an injection of a gene that prevents cancer. Apparently we all have these genes but they are not always strong enough.

The questionnaire looks at ethnic origin. I tick Ashkenazi Jewish; it is more than likely the reason that I have the cancer. There is a genetic pre-disposition in that group. That is frightening in itself.

There are delays with everyone's medication today. I have to stay on the glucose drip an extra hour. A seventy-seven year-old man that I spoke to three weeks ago is told he has to wait another two hours for his chemo, so he sits at my bedside and starts talking to me.

"I have learnt so much from you," he says. "I can't talk to other people because they haven't a clue where I'm coming from. They say it will be alright, but what to they know?"

I find myself listening to his story. He repeats himself several times. Perhaps the 'normal' me would be bored by this, but I have all the time in the world and can help him feel better. He has had a full colostomy and finds it embarrassing to talk about to outsiders. He doesn't want to know how many lesions they found in his liver. He is surprised when

I tell him I like to know everything.

So today when I finally leave the hospital after eight hours I know that I have helped someone to feel better.

I also realise that, compared with him, I am one very lucky person.

3rd December

Though I had made up my mind not to fight the side effects this time and have had two days in pyjamas I wake up this morning feeling like a caged tiger. The pins and needles are back as soon as I get up, and my arm feels like a dead weight where the Oxaliplatin went in.

I have a long chat with my son Dan, whom I now nickname my Personal Administrator since he sorts out all my ICT glitches and steers me from Luddite tendencies. His sense of humour is a great comfort too. He is planning to come to the Island on the 26th December and will stay to early January. I really look forward to it.

My hands are still painful each morning for at least two hours before the symptoms abate. I will try and brave the outdoors later, but I am dreading it, as I know that even with hand warmers it will be painful and frustrating. I know I should just take one day at a time and not think about how much more lies ahead but that is a tough call right now. Most days I can count my blessings, but sometimes it just doesn't work and I collapse into a miserable heap. Poor Chris; he is so supportive but he has a lot on his plate right now putting up with me and these chemo-induced mood swings.

Fortunately it was relative mild outside, so the venture into the outdoors was not too daunting and I felt better for having made the effort. I think part of the problem is my expectation of feeling well as opposed to poorly. That makes it difficult to accept these painful physical reactions. The cool air, as a direct result of the chemo, contorts my face. I have to warm it up to relax the muscles. I refuse to let any of this stop me from going out.

I had a visit from an ex-colleague, Ian, who is also undergoing chemo and is awaiting a kidney transplant. It was good to talk through the stresses of coping with debilitation and illness with someone who understands and who has been through it. He also gave me some help with claims and benefits. I will start the ball rolling with some phone calls.

I am able to chat with Rachel most days and her wonderful suggestions as to how to tolerate this enforced period of sickness really help me stay upbeat. The latest suggestion is that I attempt something that doesn't require 'hands'; I should learn another language!

Despite constant application of aqueous cream my skin feels dry and scaly and as though it doesn't quite belong to me. Spontaneous splits are appearing in my fingers and make me feel once again as though I am being poisoned in some way. Though I try to view the treatment positively it is sometimes hard to achieve – even though the markers are down, reminding me that the suffering really is worthwhile.

Today I must summon the energy to make those phone calls. Motivation eludes me. I have lost my health, a degree of confidence, and some of my lifestyle. I think of the folk I have come across at times who have also been lost. There was the little boy I helped who had simply lost his way, an old man with dementia who had lost his grip on reality which plunged him into a nightmare world, and an old lady with Alzheimer's who had strayed from an old people's home.

Lost

Fourteen years-old and walking home from school one summer's evening I saw a small boy with beautiful honey-coloured skin, wearing a stripy t-shirt. He couldn't have been much older than ten. His large brown eyes were overflowing with tears. I bent down and offered him a tissue.

"What's the matter? Can I help?"

Between sniffs he stuttered out his reply: "I've been to a birthday party this afternoon and I can't find my way back!"

"Where do you live?"

"Dr Barnardo's. But I don't know where it is."

I knew the home was somewhere in Barkingside, but I had no idea which road it was in. The boy was so clearly upset I wanted to reassure him. I said, "Come back to my house. I just live up the road. I'll ring them and they can sort this out."

While he had a cold drink I managed to speak to someone at the home. With that naïve optimism of youth I simply said, "I have a small boy here who is lost."

Thinking back I wonder what kind of reaction I had expected to such a ridiculous statement. These people probably get hundreds of calls about lost children. It just didn't occur to me at the time.

"What do you expect us to do about it?" came the terse response.

"He says he lives with you…"

With that, her coldness melted. She took details and they sent a car round to my house to collect him.

I really felt for the little lad. His whole world had collapsed around him and he couldn't find his way. He must have been terrified.

Many years later I came across another 'stray'. A little old lady wandered up our drive and managed to get into our back garden. She was clearly disorientated and didn't have a clue who she was or where she came from. Not wanting to put my children at risk (they were then aged about ten and twelve) I walked her round to the local shops from where we called the police. I found out later that she had wandered from an old people's home.

The most distressing case was a man in the bed next to my Mum at the London Hospital. He was terribly upset. He believed himself to be at a busy station and kept grabbing nurses and visitors and begging them to help him. "Please tell me how I can get home," he would plead. "I'm lost. Which train do I catch…?"

No matter how many times he was reassured that he was safe and in hospital, within minutes he was re-living his constant nightmare.

Diary – 7th December 2007

Today I sit next to a dying man in the Chemo Suite. He has cancer of the oesophagus. It is incurable and Dr B is giving him chemotherapy to prolong his life. He has little more than a year to live. His wife is devastated. He also has a five year-old granddaughter. They are giving her a book written by Sarah Ferguson entitled Saying Goodbye to Grandpa.

I feel choked. When I look at him he has death written in his face. I recognise it. Now when I look in the mirror at my own face, I see only life. I can't help wondering if that will change in the near or distant future.

I have made the phone call to Job Centre Plus and my claim for incapacity benefit is hopefully winging its way to Southampton.

The steroid injection I had yesterday causes me to wake at 3am. I read for two hours and still can't fall back to sleep so I give up and get up. Yesterday I had another 'cook-in' in the kitchen. I can't stomach any type of milk at the moment and Rachel suggested I bake muesli bread. I have some for breakfast and it goes down well.

Two hours later I feel nauseous, but that is a common side effect of eating at the moment. There is always a cost!

I have received a Christmas card from the parent of one of the emotionally and behaviourally disturbed teenagers that I was working with intensively for two years.

Her comment brings tears to my eyes.

"Thank you for all your support with my daughter over the last three years. All the time in helping her with her social skills and learning skills. Also helping myself and just being a phone call away. Always having the time to listen and offer advice. I hope you are getting better soon."

This is her daughter's final year at the school. It is strange to contemplate never working with her again. I have some huge adjustments to make in my life. It is daunting.

Working with Clara

Clara came to the high school on a pre-visit in the July preceding her entry to High School and from that moment I knew it would be a rocky ride with her. She was clearly not able to cope with the huge transition from Middle School and made me the focus of her extreme anger fear and frustration.

She glared at me venomously, and began screaming: "I'm not staying in this room with THAT woman". Her menacing finger was directed exclusively at me. Clearly her Mum was embarrassed to extremes and gradually manipulated her out of the room and away from the situation.

When Clara joined us in September her anger was on constant simmer and would boil over with little provocation. The windows needed to be open (she suffered with urtacaria, red itchy skin), the classrooms were too warm, the teachers were unfair.

When we examined each of the issues it soon became clear that Clara could not cope within a mainstream classroom, so we adopted her in our small support area and gradually Clara learned how to control her anger. Handled sensitively she began to trust us. She came with an attachment disorder making it painfully difficult for her to bond with adults. Her birth mother was only thirteen years-old when she had Clara and the lack of pre-natal care caused physical difficulties: a speech impediment, plus complex health and learning difficulties. Clara was now adopted, but it had proved tough for her adoptive mother to cope with the temper tantrums and the attachment disorder. Both she and Clara needed enormous support just to cope from day to day.

Over the course of two years Clara was transformed. Patience and understanding of her specific needs led to huge improvements. Clara had a passion for horses and we were able to find her a work experience placement at a local stables where her expertise and knowledge helped her towards an NVQ.

The boost to her self-esteem impacted on her general behaviours and by the time I became ill Clara was a calmer happier young lady.

She was very upset when I went off sick in July and when I didn't reappear in September she found it difficult to accept the loss of her 'key worker'.

Diary– 11th December 2007

Every day I find copious amounts of skin in my clothing. I warn Chris that he may one morning wake to find an empty outer shell, shaped like me but with nothing inside it.

I have always had really thick wiry hair (the grandchildren call it Grandma's sharp hair), but now I am noticing bits of scalp showing through. They warned me it was a side effect of the chemo, though I am unlikely to go completely bald with this particular drug. I must be grateful for that.

The furniture arrived this morning as promised just before eleven and it is a blessing to relax into a comfy reclining settee rather than perch awkwardly in a garden chair which I've been doing for the last month!

The delivery men are helpful and unpack it all for me, taking the mess with them. Great! It would have taken me the rest of the day in my current state. I express my gratitude with a tip. At Rachel's request I send some pictures of the couches to her via email. By return she sends me some snaps of the girls with the comment, "Sorry, my kids don't look quite as comfy and luxurious as your couches, but I think you'll agree they are much cuter!"

Another week on from the treatment and today we will brave the supermarket again. This trip should be more successful as the neuropathy is far less extreme, though it is quite cold outside (nothing compared with Ottawa , but pretty cold for the UK). Ottawa could save a fortune in meteorological reporting if they adopted Rachel's delightfully simple descriptions of Canadian winter temperatures. She has honed it to two possibilities: "Minus a bit, or minus a lot."

It is plus six degrees here. I shouldn't complain.

I take in a tin of biscuits and Christmas cards for the nurses. They appreciate the fact that I wrote individual messages to each of them.

Cerys tries three times to put a needle in and fails.

Then Kate has a go. It takes over half an hour and my hand is black and blue.

Minna takes a look at my rash and flaky skin and calls the doctor in. They think it is a side effect of the anti-body (Cetuximab) and they write a prescription for more antibiotic lotion plus antihistamine tablets. Minna tells me that my reaction to the drug is a really good sign. It means that more likely than not, it is working!

They are planning to schedule the scan for early January (when the treatment has completed full cycle) This means that they will more than likely operate in early February. The next bout of chemo may well begin in March. I can't help needing to know what will happen. Control freaks are like that! Clearly the dates are an estimation and subject to some change; we will see. Minna is referring me to the Macmillan Cancer Nurses for extra support through all this treatment.

I have a bad night thanks to the steroid. I was awake for hours thinking about the future. Yesterday I met a colleague in the suite. She has had two successive treatments for breast cancer but the tumour has grown back so she has to endure a third cycle with a new drug. Her hair had recovered, but she has now lost it all again. I look at her and I wonder if I could cope with the idea of even more chemo. I just pray that won't happen to me, but I can't help but feel it is all out of my hands and I have to surrender to whatever will be. I can stay positive and believe in a good outcome, but deep down I know nothing is certain. It is a frightening thought.

To cheer me up I am having my kitchen re-designed, making good use of existing cupboards. We have lived without a dishwasher for the past seven years, but I think the time has come to treat myself. I certainly don't want to spend what time I have at the kitchen sink! So an exciting prospect for the New Year. The kitchen design company is coming today to discuss finer details. When Karl came to measure up a few weeks ago, he had been here twenty minutes and I had shaken his hand before he told us his daughter had an awful throat bug and had been ill for three weeks. He was coming down with it. I fled into another room. After he left I gave Chris the anti–bacterial spray and he went round every kitchen surface and even sprayed the booklet Karl left us. I washed my hands thoroughly and hoped for the best. I am pleased to report I contracted a bit of a fright – but luckily no bugs! In my weakened condition it could have set me back weeks.

This morning I got a letter regarding my claim for incapacity benefit: I am returning the enclosed SSP1, as this on its own cannot be accepted as a claim to Incapacity Benefit.

I am really irritated since I had been told to simply send in the SSP1. I telephone the Job Centre Plus and ask for an explanation. A very pleasant man tells me that now all claims are handled on the telephone and he is mystified as to why I was given the wrong information. I spend nearly half an hour on the phone answering a myriad of questions about my job, my illness and any previous claims I might have made. Now I have to wait until he sends me the statement we have completed so that I can sign and return it with the original SSP1. The bouncing back and forth of the identical claim form seems an inordinate waste of time and money. The resultant delay may mean that the claim will not go through before my pay is reduced by half.

So much for bureaucracy. I am not a happy bunny and could do without the additional stress.

21st December

When I see Dr B he is once again pleased with my progress.

He tells me that my liver enzymes are raised, showing that there is irritation in the liver, but he would expect that given the tumours. They are slightly less elevated than they were at the start.

I will have to decide whether I can cope with four more Chemo sessions after the operation. I don't have to decide yet, but he knows that sometimes it is too difficult to tolerate. We will have to see how well I recover. Apparently a few years ago they would not have operated at all and there would have been no possibility of a cure. The surgery is more advanced nowadays and they are learning new techniques all the time. He expects the scan to be in the second week of January and the operation to be early February. Then there will be a month's recovery before Chemo. Dr B reassures me that the tumours will still be responding to the first bout so there should not be any risk of them growing back in that short space of time. He thinks I am continuing to respond well to treatment. Minna makes a provisional appointment for me to see Dr B again on January seventeenth but if the operation and scans are all set I may not need to attend. The surgeons in Southampton may want to see me in advance of the operation.

I wish I could be given more concrete dates; I hate the way everything hangs in the air, but there is nothing more I can do now.

It is Rachel's birthday and for the first time ever I didn't have a chance even to speak to her. I have been stuck at the hospital all day.

This is the last chemo before the op and the veins in my right arm were not co-operating. The first needle burst the vein wall and fluid leaked into the surrounding tissue. Maria couldn't then use a larger needle so the drip was painful for two hours. Now my arm feels like a dead weight and is agony. I can't use it at all. Both Minna and Maria tell me my arm would not tolerate another dose of Oxaliplatin. The effects are cumulative.

Good news is that my CEA marker is now down to 42.2. For the next few days I will have to grin and bear the side effects.

Shaun, a colleague fom school pops in for a brief visit en route to our neighbours Nigel and Ella. He brings me a Harrod's Christmas hamper; a gift from the staff. Apparently I was mentioned at the end of term farewell gathering and everyone clapped. I should be able to pop in and visit them in January one the infection risk from the chemo diminishes.

Dan arrives on Sunday which is great. When on earth did my children grow to be so sensible?

Kids

Rachel was born in 1976 in South Africa. She was a beautiful baby, with navy blue eyes and a shock of dark hair, which she then lost and which grew back blond.

Perhaps because of the bonding problems I had, she grew up with a lot of insecurities. Like most children she took things very literally. Paul shouted at her one day in a panic because she put a plastic carrier bag over her head.

"You'll die if you put that on your head. Take it off now!"

Ten minutes later she was in floods of tears.

"What's the matter? Have you hurt yourself?"

"Will I…" she sobbed, "will I die now, or later?"

When she was still at primary school I volunteered to collect money for the blind, and made preparations to take the children around the local streets with me.

Rachel tugged my arm urgently: "But Mummy, where are we going to find all those blind people?"

Daniel was two years younger. He was fairer than his sister and a very contented baby who only cried when tired or hungry. He was always very sensitive as a small child and it is because of his persistence that we eventually welcomed a cat, Whiskey, into our family.

For years I had repeatedly told my children, "If an animal comes to stay in this house, I go, and that is final!" When they realised that no amount of nagging, whining or pleading would bring me to surrender, the message sank in. Mother would not allow anything of the winged, feathered or four-legged variety into the home.

Thankfully the matter was dropped – or so it seemed.

I really felt that with a full-time job and two children under ten, I had enough to cope with just running the house. As it was, leaving home each morning was like *The Great Escape*. Leaking flasks, keys that hid themselves, tears, forgotten books and bags…

I was adamant. No animals!

My suspicions should have been aroused when eight year-old Daniel surreptitiously helped himself to one of his sister's cornflakes at breakfast. Knowing his appetite, I didn't pay very much attention. When the poaching of cornflakes became a well -established behaviour pattern I casually asked.

"What do you want cornflakes for, Daniel?"

There followed the familiar lowering of his eyes combined with a pronounced guilty grin. "Nothing," came his bold reply.

I repeated the question more firmly. His resistance crumbled and there was no further attempt at evasion.

"It's... it's for my ant." He muttered the answer so rapidly that I hardly absorbed its content.

"Your *what?*" I queried in disbelief.

"My ant."

"What ant?" I enquired calmly attempting to suppress rising panic.

"'My pet ant."

"Oh." I swallowed. "And where is this... this pet ant?"

I should have guessed. My poor deprived son had resorted to keeping an ant in his bedroom as a pet, and feeding it Rachel's cornflakes. Gently I explained why I had to evict the ant from the premises. I talked about colonies, the increase of the species and how the ant might just have been tempted to invite his family in to take up permanent residence in the kitchen. Eventually I was able to convince him that ants belong in the garden. I must have sounded convincing. My voice had become quite shrill.

A few nights later when Daniel went to feed his pet, to his horror he discovered that it had passed away. He was shaken. Not even the ensuing conversation about that great anthill in the sky could diminish his grief.

He earnestly set to work building a huge ant complex on the garden path. I would have encouraged his interest in natural history more enthusiastically had he not purloined my desk tidy as his 'starter kit'. The five ants he housed in it perished before morning. I explained patiently about the need for air holes. The next colony survived the first day, and then in the night there was a rainstorm. The following day was a scene of devastation. All the lids had blown off, and the inmates – seizing their opportunity – had escaped.

The ant craze lasted until the end of the summer, when a swarm of flying ants invaded the garden. It seemed to serve as an adequate deterrent. Life was not easy after that. Every comment or reference to living creatures evoked sighs of longing.

One day, on finding biscuit crumbs on Daniel's carpet I shouted, "Look at this mess… do you want mice?"

His eyes lit up.

"Yes," he replied innocently. My guilt trip intensified.

Following the ants, we went through buckets of tadpoles, a baby frog, several spiders, some undesirable worms. Daniel was not interested in the pet rock I suggested. What choice did I have? I relented. We went to the Cats Protection League and brought home a kitten. I was tempted to name her 'Final'.

Daniel always had the most incredible imagination and would invent all sorts of off-the-wall things for his bedroom. He erected a pulley in the bunk bed that enabled him to hoist up a glass of water from bottom to top bunk. It worked brilliantly until the cardboard and string broke, causing a cascade of water to waken him in the night. His sense of humour developed from a really young age. Rachel loved to tell tales about him and came bursting into the kitchen when he was around eight years-old:

"Mummy, Daniel took a drink and a biscuit without asking."

"Did you, Daniel?"

He nodded sheepishly.

"It's polite to ask before taking things," I said.

"But I knew you would say 'yes' so I didn't think it would matter."

As they got older they both become cannier. In preparation for moving house from Cobden Road I was methodically clearing out each room. I came across some red Dymo tape just under the top-most kitchen cupboard. It was neatly printed with the words *Random Crap We Never Use.*

Daniel had got hold of the Dymo and the children had gone round the house sticking them all over the place. We were all fond of the song about Lowrie that was popular in the Eighties, *Matchstalk Men.* Rachel had misheard the line, *He takes his brush and he waits, outside those factory gates...*

She used to sing: "He takes his pressurny weights..."

When I went to pack my pressure cooker, I found the weights also had a piece of Dymo tape applied to them, and they were now renamed: PRESSURNY WEIGHTS.

Diary – 25th December 2007

My incapacity benefit telephone statement arrived yesterday. I checked it over and added the dates of each of the five hospital admissions. The claim will be back-dated if it is late, which is useful to know.

This is the worst reaction to treatment I have had so far. My arm is so painful and tender I can hardly move it. The pins and needles in my hands and feet make it difficult for me to do even the simplest activities, and I have been unable to venture out for two days.

It is great to see Dan, and I intend to make the best of the time we have, despite the limitations imposed on me by Oxaliplatin. The way I feel at the moment I don't think I could tolerate another dose, either emotionally or physically so it is a good thing there is a break from it now.

This time, as well as his technological expertise, Dan has brought bags full of chocolate; gifts from his pupils and the staff at the school. He couldn't possibly manage to eat it by himself, and wondered if Chris would help. Chris was unpacking box after box with a beatific smile on his face. A chocaholic's heaven. Whilst he did that Dan showed me how to join Facebook. Paul's comment: "Every time Dan comes to visit you, you seem to take an exponential step up the greasy ladder of technology."

Very apt... and yes, when Dan returns to Leeds, I'm afraid I might slip right down the rungs again.

Now Dan tells me that on Facebook I can throw sheep at people or give them zombie bites.

I really don't feel I belong in this strange world...

We have had lots of fun today playing silly games. On the way back from our walk we made up limericks, one line each. We played Charades, and Humbug (which is a humming game to guess the tune), followed by virtual tennis baseball and various other games on Dan's 'Wii'. The walk across the Duver was very wet but the temperatures were mild enough. The only signs of a 'white Christmas' were the foaming waves.

It was all hands to the deck when it came to lunch; mainly because I can't touch anything from the fridge. It's been a good day, marred only by my painful hands and the fact that Dan has been feeling poorly with a sore throat and a mild temperature. I am hoping not to catch the bugs.

28th December

It is Dan's birthday today and we have our traditional celebratory breakfast where he opens presents and cards. While he munches through lovingly-prepared toast and marmalade he has to tolerate my rendering of the birthday song which could be in any key with considerable variations depending on how well my voice holds up.

We go to the Chemo Suite together for the anti body drug and Dan keeps me entertained by dragging me kicking and screaming into the technological world of mobile phones as I acquaint myself with my new one. I can now text successfully... it's only taken three years.

The session goes well, though they have to use my left hand. Luckily Daniel serves as a useful substitute for my all-singing, all-dancing left arm that is indisposed for the duration. It is great to have his company and the time flies by.

I speak to Rachel on the phone and am entertained by today's asides which consist of such gems as: "Batsheva's going into the cupboard!" "No! we don't have chocolate for breakfast" and "Batsheva's chewing a dirty rag."

29th December

Dan and I are becoming a formidable pair in the boxing and tennis championships. I fare less well on the 'Wii' fitness programme and am ashamed when my virtual fitness age turns out to be seventy!

My hands are not quite so painful. Nine days on before I notice even a slight improvement.

Chris has been observing Dan's technological wizardry, and has balked at the post. I quote:

Chris:I think I'd like to return to papyrus and pencil.

Me: I don't think they had pencils then.

Dan: No it was far too advanced a technology.

Dan fiddles around on my computer and manages to acquire a voice to read my emails for times when I am too tired to open my eyes. I can't imagine I will ever need this facility but, like it or not, the disembodied Steven Hawking computer voice reads them out for me in a phoney American robotic accent. Very strange.

A frightening dream again last night. I have to make a long arduous trip several times to complete a really important task. Each journey involves travelling through a small enclosed and very dark tunnel. I don't mind reaching the destination and am relieved, but I dread going through the tunnel. It makes me feel claustrophobic and frightened. It encloses me to the point where I can hardly breathe. We move through it on some kind of train, really slowly, and I feel as if the walls are shutting me in. I have a strong urge to get away. I know that I can't reach the destination without going through the tunnel.

The meaning of the dream is immediately obvious to me when I wake up. The journey represents my chemotherapy treatments. Though I am reasonably confident of the end result, the process is a nightmare.

Daniel drives us into Ryde and we take him out for his 'birthday' lunch. We have a walk around the harbour first and then go on to an authentic Northern Italian restaurant, Michelangelo. The food is delicious. We share starters and dessert, but manage a main course each. I try the Gnocchi Pomadoro, which is lovely. Chris goes for a chicken dish and Dan has a Giovanni Pizza.

Well, I have finally come across modern terminology that Dan has never heard of. I receive an email from a French website I contacted addressing me as an 'Internaut'. What a wonderful word; a cross between an internet user and an astronaut or cybernaut!

Lots of people are thinking about 2007, and looking to the future. This year has been one of the most difficult of my life to date. I know *that I still have a very long way to go before I can return to any sort of normality. I am hospital and treatment dependent. It restricts how far and when I can travel, and how much I can accomplish in a day. That has been a monumental adjustment. I am not sure if I will ever feel comfortable with all this, and just manage from day to day. It has been terrific to have the love, support and friendship of so many to help me through. Without that, I may well have stumbled at the first hurdle.*

In 1991 I faced a huge challenge when my marriage of seventeen years fell apart. It was a different sort of struggle.

Cobden Road

At the edge of the busy A21 in Orpington, behind a large fence littered with arthritic supermarket trolleys, about fifty feet from the main road sits the large Edwardian Cottage with its low wooden beams. Stripped of furniture as it is on this day in 1991, it seems vast and empty.

Upstairs in the bedroom, all that is left are the fitted wardrobes with louvered doors lending an air of space to the magnolia room. Splitting up with Paul is traumatic for us all. The three of us sit on the double bed sobbing until we suddenly look at each other and our tears turn to laughter as we appreciate how funny we must look. We have a group hug.

Downstairs, the pink carpet, once clean, cosy and giving the front room an air of calm and peace, is now stained like blotting paper with children's activities, specks of dirt ingrained – small spots in the carpet, huge stains in the marriage.

It is early autumn and the leaves are falling in the large back garden. This had been a magical place for the children. Alive with trees and secluded as it was, we could block out traffic noise in our heads and were able to imagine being in our own private forest. We'd shared some amusing and poignant moments.

The cat, Whiskey, had fallen into the pond whilst trying to hook a goldfish with eager paws. She jumped out in terror on all four legs, fur spiky like some sort of electrocuted monster from the deep. Whiskey wore a magnetic collar to operate the cat flap. It worked really efficiently in keeping unwanted pets from entering the house, but the side effects were sometimes hilarious; the collar attracted small magnetic objects that stuck to it, and we would have to rescue her, pulling off random items she had collected on her travels which sometimes weighed her down almost to the ground.

How we had laughed when Rachel burst into our room one morning: "Mummy come quickly the taps are talking!"

She'd dragged me into the bathroom insisting it was true. I suspended extreme scepticism and not wanting to hurt her feelings went to investigate the problem.

As I bent down to the taps I heard a low nasal exchange of voices. For a split second I too believed in the impossible until I noticed the sound was emanating from the radio, behind the basin. The battery had almost run down, and the voices were scarcely discernible like old men commiserating together.

One morning at five Rachel's screams of terror woke me from a deep slumber; there was no time to speculate on whether or not she was hurt, under attack, or worse. I flew into her room as fast as I could, eyes ripped from my sleep state, alert and ready for anything.

When I opened the door I immediately took in the scene. Rachel was cowering under the bedclothes whilst a panicked baby blackbird was flapping its wings and crashing into all the furniture. Whiskey was on her haunches, shoulders protruding like daggers, ready to pounce, enjoying the chase.

As Rachel made her escape into my bedroom and I booted out the huntress, I tried to catch the terrified fledgling before it completely covered her bookshelves bed and window-sill with bird's doddle. Not easy. In the end a towel thrown over the tiny creature allowed me to release it into the open where the parents, like Banshees, were screeching in unison. That story at least had a happy ending.

Rachel, Daniel and I were desperate to remain in the house when their Dad wanted to sell. The potential purchasers pulled out and, as the year went on, the bathroom tiles began crumbling and gradually dropped off. The outside lintel leaked chronically each time it rained and we needed at least four buckets under the patio window in the lounge to catch the drips. The utility room roof was starting to cave in, the plaster heavy with damp like sodden cardboard. Though the building had always been structurally sound when the marriage worked, by the time we had split up, and the feel was of a shallow empty crumbling shell; a reflection of the failing relationship. It was as if the property was communicating with us, persuading us to leave.

Now that the removal day had finally arrived we could hardly wait to escape and turn over a fresh page in our lives.

When we left Cobden Road in Farnborough Village following the divorce, the three of us moved to Sparrow Drive. I loved the road. I had found a property to purchase there the year before, but then our own house sale had fallen through. I was bitterly disappointed. Even though I knew we had lost the property in Sparrow Drive, each time I drove past the street I had an irresistible urge to indicate right and turn into that road. Daily I had to force myself to keep driving. It was a wrench.

We continued to look at properties in various locations, all of which were a disappointment. Finally, a year on, our Cobden Road house was sold, and another property came up in Sparrow Drive. I was lucky. The housing market had collapsed and this one was £10,000 cheaper! It was a Sixties build – a town house on three storeys. Though terraced it was solidly built and quiet. It had a small manageable back garden with a footpath leading to Sparrow Wood.

If I was on the top floor I could hear nothing from the floors below which made it an ideal house to share with two teenagers. For me it signalled my independence. 'He' had never lived there. It was mine.

The house was vacant when we viewed it. It needed little

maintenance and just a lick of paint and some new flooring to replace the vomit-coloured carpet. Single-handedly I covered the dull brown paint with pale grey and lightened the upstairs with some white emulsion. Rachel decorated her own room, choosing purple and yellow gloss for the paintwork, and green sponging on the pastel walls.

It was 'our' house and we put our unique stamp on it.

We lived there for nine happy years. It was warm and welcoming, with a gentle atmosphere.

Diary – January 1st 2008

We had a great sing song last night, with guitars, keyboard and harmonica. We ate home made pizzas and just before midnight some hot home-baked doughnuts dipped in melted butter and icing sugar. I felt a little disheartened as the new year arrived. Will it herald anything worth looking forward to?

Playing Sixties music took me back to the time when I first heard the Beatles. Grandma thought they were long-haired scruffians. Mum was slightly more tolerant. That is until I bought my first single.

The Beatles

I spent my free time wearing *Richard Kimble is Innocent* t-shirts mooning over David Janssen and recording sound tracks from *The Fugitive*.

I was obsessed.

Despite my crush on various TV actors and covering my walls with their photos, I wasn't that interested in pop music until one particular Saturday evening in February 1963 when I watched *Thank Your Lucky Stars* on TV and heard an amazing sound. It was *Please Please Me* performed by a new dynamic foursome, The Beatles.

I was hooked. I could hardly wait for their next release and I saved up my pocket money until I had the necessary shillings and pence to purchase *She Loves You.* Thrilled, I rushed upstairs and put it on the record player. I set the button to eject so that it would play continuously.

That was my first single. Nowadays I can't listen to *She Loves You* without laughing aloud when I think of Mum's reaction. She was clearly driven to total distraction by the repetitiveness.

It was around the 20th 'You think you've lost your love, well I saw her yesterday' that she came bursting into my room, red in the face and close to melt down.

"Turn that awful racket off now," she commanded, "or I will smash it to bits and that contraption with it!" She waved menacingly at the large orange and cream plywood case Gerald had rigged up for me with amplifier and deck.

I was horrified. It hadn't occurred to me that she wouldn't completely share in my enjoyment and that she might not want to hear the same tune playing all afternoon.

We reached a truce and compromise after that sticky episode. Mum even began to enjoy some of the music and understood my enthusiasm. A couple of years later in January 1965 the Beatles were booked to perform at Hammersmith Odeon. My brother Gerald and cousin Michael were going to get tickets and I begged them to take me. Gerald was reluctant.

"Mum, there will be crowds of people. She could get lost. I don't think it's a good idea"

Mum fought my case. "Oh come on, she is desperate to see them. She'll stick with you the whole time. Let her go with."

I don't think Gerald was that concerned about my welfare. He just knew he'd be in deep trouble if he came back home without me, so he took control and never let me out of his sight.

We sat in the 'gods' in that huge amphitheatre, me crossing my legs because I wasn't even allowed a visit to the toilet. None of that mattered. I saw my heroes for the first time. The audience was a seething, teeth-gnashing, hair-pulling, clothes-rending, deafening mass of hysterical teenagers and I was proud to be one of them.

I screamed for Paul McCartney all the way through their set. I scarcely heard any music, and I could see Paul's face only with the help of a pair of opera glasses – I emerged with a sore throat and pounding ears, but I had seen the Beatles live. I was in heaven!

Diary – 2nd January 2008

My flaky skin feels rough, tough and uncomfortable. It leaves unsightly deposits in the bed and on the chairs. I can't use phrases like 'It's no skin off my nose' without Chris and Dan exchanging knowing looks and meaningful smiles. I shed white flakes everywhere. The resident dust mites will most probably be grossly obese by now and it won't be long before we will be able to spot them with the naked eye as they loll around the house, bulbous and sated. Does munching on my cast off epidermis equate to a daily diet of McDonald's and chips, I wonder?

Daniel drives us over to Portsmouth today. We have lunch together and say goodbye. I will miss him. We look around the shops for a short while, but the icy wind makes it difficult for me to tolerate. We soon loose heart and return home.

I have received notification of my scan in Southampton. It is on January 15th (my birthday) which means that due to some weird irony I will have spent Rachel's, Daniel's and my own birthday at the hospital this year. Is there a message for me there?

I also received a large package from Canada to 'Migramainglund' which includes Levana's stunning drawings, delightful letters and messages to me.

I shall treasure them forever.

4th January

Today is a milestone: my final session in the Chemo Suite until I resume in March or April.

Anita warns me that she has to take an extremely talkative lady for a scan first. She picks me up early. She hadn't exaggerated. The lady is pleasant enough but hardly pauses for breath regaling us with tales from her life. Her husband sits humbly on the back seat and only comes to life with three or four words when she mentions a TV programme.

Otherwise he is silent along with the rest of us. I find myself secretly wishing she had an off switch.

When we finally arrive at Chemo the car smells of old people and I am relieved to step into the fresh air. They have locked the back door of the hospital because of the prevalent Norovirus which is a sickness bug that has spread throughout the country. Everyone has to go in through the main entrance and use antiseptic hand wash.

We walk through the hospital and up to the suite with another patient who has been battling cancer for the last six years. He and I exchange stories. It is good to speak to someone who understands how upsetting it can be not even to be able to drink a glass of water. Hearing his struggle helps me once again see how lucky I am.

Though I am off the tablets this week, recovery is painfully slow and laborious. It is good to have a returning appetite, but my mouth and hands are still sore, my nose keeps bleeding, and my skin continues to flake copiously.

I need to accept all these changes to my body, but it is difficult.

I have been for a gentle walk across the Duver. I would have liked a brisker pace, but I just couldn't find the energy.

Taking Rachel's advice and with Daniel's help, I am learning Spanish. He has given me the lessons that he used and they really are well put together. It makes language learning fun and very straightforward. Hopefully Chris and I will visit his family in Lanzarote when my treatment is over and I will be able to try it out. Muy bien!

The Macmillan Nurse, Annie, visits this afternoon. She will support my application for early retirement and help with any benefit problems. She has also promised to come round after my operation.

She explains the significance of the cancer markers; they don't necessarily show whether or not the tumours have shrunk, but how active or inactive they are. The fact that the liver tests show an improvement is also promising. It is useful to speak to someone who understands all aspects of this disease.

I read something online which really resonates with me:

Courage doesn't always roar.
Sometimes courage is the
quiet voice at the end of the day saying,
"I will try again tomorrow."
(Mary Anne Radmacher)

Diary – 9th January 2008

This morning the neuropathy is considerably less troublesome, though my skin is ultra sensitive. I burnt myself three days ago just by the back of my finger momentarily touching the top of the toaster. I now have a painful blister which considering the minor nature of the injury really shouldn't be there!

Last night I had a very strange dream that I decided to stop writing my Blog. Instead of it just ending, someone else was going to take it over. That seemed to wrong to me. I wasn't at all happy with this outcome and I felt a huge sense of loss, akin to a bereavement even though it was my decision. Such strong emotions; for once I am not sure I understand the dream entirely, if at all!

When I speak to Rachel on the phone we talk it through and both hit upon the meaning simultaneously. It is to do with my job. I am choosing to give it up, but it is nevertheless a wrench to stop working with needy students, and I miss the close relationship with valued colleagues. Retirement is will be a big adjustment for me and comes on top of learning to live with cancer.

I go for a walk and buy a bottle of water, but despite being very thirsty I am unable to open it! My hands are not strong enough. I feel silly and helpless asking a complete stranger for help, but in the end my thirst gets the better of me and I ask a dog walker if she will open it. She is happy to oblige and tells me that her Gran can never open medicine bottles because of the child-proof tops that are virtually adult-proof too! Now I don't feel so bad!

The neuropathy is gone now, and it is such a relief not to have had another treatment on Friday! My first 'free' Friday in three months. I spent much of it practising my art with pastels. It is fun. I have been doing lots of drawings of animals for the kids and sending them to Canada. Rachel tells me they inspire Levana to draw, which is wonderful. My fingertips are still split and sore. I have to keep applying cream, but this discomfort is preferable to neuropathy any day!

Chris and I are planning to spend the night in Southampton the day of my scan so we can celebrate my birthday. We may even go to the theatre that night. They are showing The Wizard of Oz, *which should be fun and not too taxing. Today we walk across the Duver and find three discarded socks and some underwear. There are some strange people about!*

We booked a hotel and the theatre for Tuesday. It is the first time I have been away since the trouble began in late June. I look forward to the adventure once the scan is out of the way and I have drunk the contrast fluid, had the injection of dye and been shoved in a small tunnel for forty minutes. That bit doesn't fill me with joyous anticipation.

16th January

I had a funny sort of a birthday really. When we woke first thing to make our way to Southampton for my scan it was a dark stormy day and gushing with rain outside.

We had decided to go by bus to Cowes and take the Red Jet to Southampton as there is nowhere to safely leave a car overnight. Walking to the bus stop was a challenge since the car drivers were racing past and one of them targeted my leg with a particularly spectacular splash, so I started the day pretty wet and became progressively wetter.

The weather didn't improve much and we gave up waiting for a bus in the downpour from town to the hospital and took a taxi. Once there I had to drink a jug-full of disgusting Ribena-flavoured contrast fluid. I have had nicer drinks to celebrate a birthday!

Several people in the waiting room in Oncology were playing on their recently acquired Nintendo DS consoles and discussing their relevant scores for brain training. It looks fun and I am sorely tempted to get one, though so far without success since they seem to have sold out before Christmas and not re-stocked.

I was finally released at 12.30pm, and we caught a bus back into town. After shopping and a rest at the hotel we made our way to the Mayflower and picked up our tickets at the box office. It was an excellent production with some amazing special effects. The tornado was done with the use of background film, thunderous sound effects and lighting flashes, making the whole thing feel very real.

I think I am a big softie at heart as I am a sucker for happy endings and the idea that good will always triumph over evil. I wish that all our world's 'wicked witches of the west' would get their come-uppance in similar fashion. The audience was responsive and the atmosphere was great throughout.

We had a comfortable night in the hotel. We hadn't bothered with a meal after the show so enjoyed a lovely breakfast before walking back into town for more retail therapy.

Around midday we picked up the suitcase and wended our way back to the ferry terminal. It was a simple enough journey home. The water was much calmer than the outward trip and the boat skimmed smoothly back to Cowes.

Arriving home I found a pile of birthday cards on the mat... I also had email and phone messages.

17th January

St Mary's again this afternoon. I am getting so fed up with being in hospitals. I realise I have been on this treadmill of appointments, blood tests and injections for the past seven months, and I know this is only half way! I long for a time when I can be free of it all and they will finally leave me alone.

Dr B was optimistic from the blood tests that I should be in line for the operation in February. He says that he will be discussing yesterday's scan with the liver surgeons next Wednesday, and I should receive a letter inviting me for an appointment to see them and possibly with a date for surgery. So I play the waiting game again.

Minna says that the chemo is likely to stay in my system for weeks, which is why I still have the skin problems and splitting fingers. For this reason they are giving me a break from chemo before surgery. Dr B says the pre-surgery chemo is far more important than post surgery so if I can't tolerate four more it shouldn't make much difference to the outcome.

I try to make the most of these hospital trips by doing a bit of shopping prior to the visit, which dilutes the boring predictability of it all.

It seems Carisbrooke High, my place of work for the past seven years, is closing after all. They have been prevaricating about making any final decisions, but now the council have decided the site will be used for a new faith school and all the staff will have to re-apply for jobs within the authority, whatever happens to Island education. No doubt I will need to discuss my position with the Head, which I plan to do when I visit the school towards the end of the month.

It all feels very wierd, but it is strangely comforting to know my work situation would have changed even if I hadn't got ill.

Worry

I have always been an anxious sort of person and as a child I worried about absolutely everything. Every night before going to sleep I had to get Mum to check there were no skeletons hiding under the bed. I would turn around dozens of times on the stairs to make sure no one was following me. It became so extreme that it almost developed into an obsessive compulsive disorder. I wouldn't settle to sleep until I had checked that every drawer in the room was tightly shut (the monsters might otherwise seep out in the night). Luckily my wonderful Grandma helped me overcome the worst symptoms with her timely advice: "Just say 'no' and pray to the angels to protect you."

It worked.

As I developed the anxieties translated from childish fears into realistic worries. Would the house be burgled? Catch fire? Flood?

Would there be a third world war?

Worrying about what might happen filled my life with uncertainty. I recognised it wasn't healthy but neither was it easy to control.

Hearing the following anecdote helped me a lot...

A woman went on holiday and spent the whole two weeks abroad worrying about the house being burgled.

When the family returned the house was fine. She went to put a chicken in the oven and the oven exploded!

It dawned on me that constantly worrying doesn't prevent disaster.

Recently I had been concerned about global warming, terrorism , Sars, Bird Flu... not difficult nowadays to find endless issues to occupy the mind. Then in July I suddenly found out I had cancer and it was advanced.

So what have I learnt from this...?

There is absolutely no point in dwelling on what might be. Taking every precaution against burglary, theft, etc is worth it. But worrying when you can't change things makes no impact on reality. None of us knows what is round the corner. If I had my time again I would live much more in the moment. As J T O'Hara affirms in his book *And Other Tidbits for Living the Good Life*:

"Trust in God but lock your car."

Diary – 21st January 2008

I wake this morning hoping that the side effects are now abating, but my nose bleeds as it has every day for months, my fingers are still splitting and a small cut in my thumb, which appeared spontaneously, refuses to heal. I worry as to how well I can recover from major surgery in this state. I can only hope that things will improve before February!

I have an email today from Jo, the Colorectal Nurse Specialist. She wrote, I've just heard from Southampton following their multidisciplinary meeting when they reviewed your scans. They have decided to send you for embolisation and then resection of your liver. I understand they are going to send you an appointment next week with Professor P to discuss this.

Jo isn't certain what an 'embolisation' is.

22nd *January*

The kitchen people start on Monday, which is great. It means I will be able to clear the cupboards while I am reasonably fit and it will all be done before the operation.

Good timing!

I also have a letter informing me that my claim for Incapacity Benefit has been accepted, which is helpful.

Today I popped into the GP surgery to ask for a further sick note. This feels so strange to me. Last night I looked up embolisation on the internet and found out all sorts of things I wish I hadn't! Apparently liver failure is not uncommon after a major resection.

I have an appointment now to see Professor P on Monday 28th, in Southampton.

I wasn't at all worried at the prospect of this operation, as I knew it would be the only way to save my life. Now I am not so sure! Hopefully it will all be explained when I see the surgeon.

A few days ago I aquired a secondhand Nintendo from Ebay. I wonder if they do a brain assessment that measures fear? Mine will be off the scale.

Once again I will be unable to drive; it was such a relief to get behind the wheel once more after such a long stretch of time.

Cars

I didn't have a single official driving lesson, but Mum taught me from scratch in her blue Mini. She was amazingly thorough and patient, and took me out every night to practise my skills. I still remember her attempts to help me master that evasive 'Road Sense'.

I would ask panicked questions, like, "Mum what shall I do with this bus?"

She gently explained that each bus was different.

"If it is indicating to pull out, you wait. If it is stationary, and you can safely overtake, then do so."

This worked fine in most situations, but shortly before I was due to take my test (and whilst driving along Wanstead Flats one evening in the gloom) my question changed to, "Mum, what shall I do with this cow?"

Thanks to her endless patience and superb tuition, I passed my test first time at age seventeen.

The nearest I came to an accident was in my early years of marriage, in the first three months of a pregnancy and with new job. I was commuting daily from our house in Maidenhead to Willesden along the busy M4. On this particular morning I was on the outside lane doing around 60mph. It was rush hour and there was a lot of traffic. Suddenly one of my tyres burst and I instinctively knew I should not try to apply the brakes. I indicated left and pulled across two busy lanes of cars. I came to a stop on the hard shoulder. I was shaking with fear. I knew that it was a miracle that neither the baby nor I had been harmed in any way.

I was just about to search for my AA key which would have enabled me to access the motorway telephone, when a red sports car pulled up behind me, and a young man got out offering to change my wheel for me. I was so flabbergasted I could scarcely do more than open the boot for him and mutter a 'thank you'. I didn't even ask his name.

Sometimes I think there are angels among us.

When their Dad left us in 1990 I had to ferry the children around in my Fiat 126, which was really a motorbike engine masquerading as a car. The boot was at the front and was very shallow. There were momentous decisions to be made about each journey. If Rachel wanted to take her guitar then Daniel had to stay behind. On dark rainy nights the windscreen wipers lacked motivation and slowed almost to a stop. They sighed painfully before attempting a lethargic swipe at the droplets of water on windscreen. Minutes passed before they would half-heartedly have another try. That was bad enough, but at the same time the headlights dimmed dangerously and the radio faded to a pathetic whisper.

The children teased me unmercifully about it, and I knew that 'Fifi' had probably had her day. It was clear that we needed a vehicle more suited to our needs.

We bought a VW Polo, whilst Mum and Dad purchased a red Honda Civic Automatic in the Eighties sometime, I don't exactly remember when. Mum adored the car because it had power steering, which was innovative in those days. Given she wasn't too mobile by then it really helped her. Dad didn't drive it that much because he never properly progressed from the kangaroo hops of the Ford Popular in the Fifites, though he somehow managed to pass his test. How he ever achieved this we will never really know. He was the sort of driver that wore a flat cap, never went faster than 25mph, and wondered why there were so many accidents around him. In fact he probably caused most of them by his hesitant driving and appalling skills!

I used the Honda myself when Mum was very ill, because I had to drive from Kent to Essex on a regular basis, so Dad said that I could use the automatic, and he would look after my VW for me. I got used to driving an automatic for the first time and really enjoyed the freedom of not worrying about gear changes.

When Dad was in hospital he asked me to take it for regular drives. I was staying in his flat then and had travelled up by train so it was really convenient. Dad loved his car. He had had an accident in it and the insurance company had decided it was a write off, but Dad absolutely insisted they repair it, so he managed to get it back after the accident and kept it several more years.

By the time Dad died Gerald wasn't interested in the Honda It was very old by then, and I had traded 'Fifi' for my VW, so I knew that the best thing to do would be to give it to Daniel. Dad would have been chuffed to bits. Daniel was training to be a teacher and could not have afforded a car of his own so it was wonderful to pass it on to him. He now had an incentive to take driving lessons and pass his test. He drove Dad's car for a couple of years and also loved it, despite its age.

Unfortunately where he lived at the time was a rough area and some youngsters broke into the car, tried to 'hot rod' it and in doing so wrecked it. This time the insurance company would not repair it and said it was worth only £500. Daniel contested the sum and managed to get them to agree it was worth £1000, which he put towards a new car with help from his Dad. He now has another more modern Honda Civic, but we both mourned the death of that red car together. It had brought so much into our lives and we knew how upset Dad would have been if he had lived to find out what ultimately happened to his treasured possession.

Diary – 23rd January 2008

I have heard from Jo again. She has sent me an email explaining about embolisation. It doesn't sound much fun. A local anaesthetic is given in the groin then a small cut is made in the skin of the groin and a thin flexible tube (catheter)is placed through the skin into the femoral artery. The catheter is threaded up the femoral artery until its tip reaches the hepatic artery. Once it is in place, tiny balls of starch or very small gelatin sponge capsules are injected. These slow down or block the blood supply to the cancer. It's all done in Radiology. Patients usually stay in for a couple of days and usually have a scan a week or so later.

When I speak to Minna I find out that the CEA marker is down to 22.2 which is good news. She can tell me nothing about the embolisation; she wasn't aware it was happening. Once again I worry at the lack of communication between the surgeons in Southampton and the oncology team on the Island. I am still feeling unsettled about the procedure. It makes it difficult to sleep soundly as the early morning hours are my most vulnerable moments.

My skin is still peeling prolifically. I am concerned as I think some of it might inadvertently end up in our food! Chris isn't bothered; he says it will give it 'body'. Yes, perhaps... in more ways than one!

I receive a letter from the Benefit office. It is bizarre, and a beautiful example of bureaucracy gone mad. "I am now writing to inform you that your Incapacity Benefit is taxable from 17.01.08. This means that when we apply the tax code of 522L (which we hold for you) to your benefit, we will be deducting tax at £0.00 per week from your gross rate..."

25th January

A busy day today! I go shopping early for some food; some simple things for next week, given that the kitchen will be out of action. I then sort out my sick note from the surgery. Confusing messages. The lady I spoke to originally at County Hall asked me to send it directly to her. On the back of the form it said that benefit claimants should post the form to the Job centre or Department of Social Security. School request I send the certificates to them. I telephone County Hall for clarification. Gill tells me that I should post it to her; she will inform school that she is sending it on to the Job Centre. Sorted!

I walk up to the pillar box realising just as I arrive that I have forgotten the stamp. All this Brain Training hasn't done much to improve my current absent-mindedness. To clear my head I walk across the Duver and back. At least it is dry and there is an approximation of sunshine.

I receive another email from Jo. She thinks the operation is likely to be within a week or so of the embolisation. I just have to wait until Monday to find out when and how they will do it. I don't find waiting easy. It has been a long day and a painfully long seven months.

The Great Outdoors

As a child I spent many hours at home with my head buried in a book. For some reason, perhaps growing up in concrete Stratford, I had little appreciation of the countryside. Nowadays I feel more in touch with my surroundings and have had my most creative and inspirational moments outside on my bike or swimming in the sea. There is something magical about the rhythm of the pedals, the gentle whir of the wheels as I ride a country lane or quiet cycle track. For me there is nothing to beat the silken salt water on my skin and the feeling of being gently enveloped by the sea. When trapped indoors in the summer I am a caged tiger, frustrated that I am missing the fresh air and sunshine. Many a summer's day I have had to spend cooped up in a building whilst at work, looking enviously at the birds enjoying their freedom, and becoming increasingly more resentful at what I was missing. The exhilaration of skating on a frozen lake or skiing through a snow covered nature reserve is second to none. When I engage in such activities I feel at one with my world.

Diary – 28th January 2008

We decide to go to Southampton via Ryde this time. We arrive at Portsmouth Harbour and get on the train to Southampton Central which is leaving from Platform three within five minutes. Once we are on the train the doors are locked and several people ask if the train is going to Waterloo.

When the train doesn't leave at the appointed time we become suspicious. Once the doors are unlocked, we check the platform computer indicator. The Southampton train has been cancelled and the train we are on is being diverted to Waterloo. Had we not looked, we would have taken an extremely circuitous route!

We are directed to take the train from Platform 5 to Fareham, and to change there for Southampton Central. There is a twenty minute wait for the train and yet another twenty minute wait in Fareham. Because of a a further cancellation we end up getting the Cardiff Central Train which is direct from Portsmouth Harbour and stops at Southampton. Ridiculous!

Once we arrive at the hospital things go a lot more smoothly. There is no wait to see the surgeon. He is very pleasant. He has a student with him who asks me lots of questions but unfortunately doesn't listen to any of my answers. I tell her I was taken back into hospital three times following colon surgery, only to be asked two minutes later: "Did you have any complications following the operation?" If this is the calibre of our future surgeons I despair.

Professor P explains that the scans show the tumours have not shrunk as dramatically as they would have liked. The operation will be very tricky as it involves removing more than the standard thirty percent of my liver. The risks are too great, which is why they need to perform an embolisation. The idea is that this will block the blood supply to the part of the liver they are removing. As a result of this procedure the remaining liver has three weeks in which to grow bigger, giving me less chance of liver failure. It seems that in 5% of cases it doesn't work.

I have a copy of the scan report. It gives a detailed description of the size of each tumour, and suggests there are some 'patches' in certain bones which show 'lucent' areas. The conclusion is that though these areas are slightly suspicious there is no clear evidence of disease elsewhere.

I will have the embolisation on Wednesday 6th February, and may have to go in the previous day – Professor P isn't sure, but the procedure has been booked. I can ring up and find out tomorrow. The major operation will follow roughly three weeks later.

I am not sure what to think. I need to face the fact that I might not survive the surgery long term, though there is a good chance I will. As a control freak I would like to know what no-one is able to tell me. That is frightening and confusing. Though I think positively about outcomes, I still need to face the possibility of the worst scenario so I am ready to meet it.

Assuming I survive the operation I could have another few years or more to live. If the cancer returns I will not undergo any further chemo. I am clear in my mind about that. This illness has taught me a lot.

29th January

I ring school today and arrange to go in and see the Head on Thursday morning. I will also speak to colleagues and visit our Student Support Centre where Julie has been battling on without me so bravely and for so long. It will feel very strange.

I also telephone Jo D, the co-ordinator for Professor P. She tells me that I will be having the embolisation on Wednesday at 1.15pm but she is unsure about when exactly I will be going in. It could be Tuesday evening. I will definitely be in on Wednesday night and should be home again by Thursday.

Hopefully she will let me know tomorrow morning.

The kitchen is progressing, though it is difficult without a sink for a few days. It was also quite cold here today, since the gas stove had to be disconnected and the boiler switched off whilst a radiator was removed. I am looking forward to the end result. The new worktops look good!

Professor P's secretary rings me. They want me at the hospital by 9am on Wednesday and I must have nothing to eat or drink six hours before the procedure. They have no bed for me until Wednesday. Clearly we would have to leave ridiculously early from here to make it on time so Chris and I decide to spend the night in a hotel in Southampton. He can then have a second night there so he can come back with me on Thursday.

31st January

It is very odd going into school today. Colleagues are pleased to see me and there are hugs and handshakes all round. Shauny talks to me about a problem class, and says afterwards he feels better already. They tell me how much they miss me and Julie introduces me to new staff as 'The Legendary Lin'. Perhaps in my absence they have glorified my achievements and forgotten all my weaknesses! Not so bad…

Then I meet with the Head who is amazingly supportive. She talks about the reorganisation of the school and tells me that she is looking to find redundancy packages for anyone over 55 if they want them, though she makes it absolutely clear that she will hold my job open for me for as long as my recovery takes. I tell her I am interested in the redundancy. We talk about an early retirement on medical grounds and she says that she will work hard with my union rep to secure both. That is very good news if if can be lined up properly. I need to have it in place within six months before my salary reduces to zero!

The Head invites the rep, Dave, into her office and he agrees to come and visit me before my operation so that we can start the ball rolling. Then the Head asks me how I am coping with these horrendous events. I explain that all the time I am looking for what messages are in this for me. She probes further and wants to know what messages I have found. I am surprised she is interested on a personal level, but it seems genuine enough. I try to be as honest as I can: "Well, I recognise that as a control freak, I cannot control everything. This illness is probably the only thing that would have stopped me continuing to work full time. I know that I need to step back, find some 'me' time and explore my creative side by painting and writing."

The question is a useful one and I think she is fascinated by the answer. Before we finish she tells me that I have made more of an impact on the school since I've been there longer than any other teacher. She is full of praise for my work, and tells me that they all miss me desperately. "We have a difficult intake this year and I know that had you been here you would have 'cracked' them by now. The others are coping but it is a struggle."

When I tell her that the operation is not without significant risk, she asks me whether I have considered how I would want to be remembered if things do go wrong; if there is anything as a school that they could do. Clearly I haven't explored that avenue, but it is food for thought.

I come away with mixed feelings – relieved that financially I am on the way to being sorted, and that my role there has been recognised. I feel a little sad that my work was brought to such an abrupt halt with no 'wind down' time. It feels very odd to know that I won't be going back. The Head assures me there would be openings for me in a much reduced capacity, maybe even as a volunteer, whatever happens to Carisbrooke.

I receive a letter from the hospital confirming next week's date for the embolisation and asking me to ring the direct dial number at the top of the letter to confirm acceptance. Why am I not surprised there is no telephone number of any description to be seen on the letter? I have to ring directory enquiries and take the scenic route.

The electrician is off sick today so the kitchen will not be properly ready until Monday. At least we can now use the sink and the washing machine.

3rd February

Have just returned from a fun weekend. Teresa, Melissa and Elliott have been planning a surprise 60th birthday party for Gerald. Between them they organised a coach to take a party of friends and family from their house in Essex to a seafood restaurant in Brighton. Teresa asked me if I could go, but I clearly couldn't promise, since I wasn't sure about the impending hospital admission. I said we might be able to meet them at the restaurant but it would be a last minute arrangement.

As it happens things worked out well and we were able to book a ferry with a view to the day in Brighton and an overnight stay with Chris's brother Andrew and his wife Nancy .

Gerald rang me on Friday, with no clue about the surprise. We chatted for ages and I smiled when he told me that Elliott and Melissa were taking him to a breakfast to celebrate his birthday… I said I hoped he would enjoy it!

Yesterday we got to Brighton in good time for the 1pm rendezvous, and went to look round the shops and lanes before walking down to Regency Square.

Gerald was so delighted to see me! He told us that he had drunk gallons of coffee that morning because Elliott and Melissa were trying to keep him from being at home until 10am to give guests the chance to arrive. Once on the coach he still didn't know where they were heading… Lakeside? Southend?

We had a great time together until their coach departed at 5pm. Then Chris and I drove on to Eastbourne and the party collapsed into the coach for the journey back. Unbeknown to Gerald there was more partying in the evening!

I am so glad that I was able to share the occasion with friends and family… it was touch and go as to whether I would be 'free' to travel.

I have to confess to feeling more than a little exhausted this evening!

4th February

We are leaving for Southampton soon. I am still anxious about the embolisation, but having the kitchen done this week is a brilliant – if expensive! – way to take my mind off it.

Now, which room shall I refurbish before the next operation…?

They finally finished the kitchen at 2.30pm yesterday afternoon and I worked until 7pm trying to get a semblance of order. I still need to go through it all at a more leisurely pace when I am recovered, but in the interim it is just great. What a delight to just go to the drawer and take out a teaspoon or to simply turn on a tap to get water. It was only a week of disruption but it felt longer.

When I went to bed last night every muscle ached but it has all been worth it!

8th February

It's over. I am home. Each time I go into hospital I remember with a jolt why I hate to be there. I have to relinquish my independence so the pain is doubled!

We have a fun time in Southampton on Tuesday buying a new kettle and waste bin to match the kitchen, and it is no problem to be at the hospital by nine the following morning. I was told in the letter to eat and drink nothing after 7am (including sweets and chewing gum). Hard to believe that anyone would munch through packets of sweets in the belief they weren't eating anything, but there is no accounting for folk!

We start off at the Admissions Ward, where they take bloods and ask the usual questions. We are then left in the waiting room for a couple of hours. The nurse tells us that the doctors will be round to explain the procedure in more detail once they have finished the ward rounds. The only doctor I see at 11.30am is of the junior species. She makes five botched attempts to insert a canula into my arm, leaving me punctured, hurt and upset. She knows absolutely nothing about the embolisation and rings for a colleague to help pierce me further. He takes one look at my reluctant veins and balks at the task ahead.

Fortunately he prevaricates with his hand-washing ceremony for so long that the nurse tells him not to bother; they will insert the drip in radiology.

At midday I am given a hospital gown and sit waiting for the porter to collect me. Chris stays by my side and is allowed to follow me to radiology where the doctor who is to perform the embolisation talks to us for well over half an hour.

He explains that it is nerve-wracking for him since the procedure is by no means straightforward. There is a fine line between the healthy and unhealthy part of my liver and too far in the wrong direction could have dire consequences. Nice!

He also goes into all the complications that could arise afterwards. I could bleed heavily and might have to have a blood transfusion. I could be in extreme pain. I sign the consent form despite all the risks. It is obvious to both of us that the alternative is far more dire and certainly inevitable. Dr S tells me not to bank on leaving hospital the following morning, but he will be happy for me to go if I feel well enough.

He stresses that they don't want 'bravery'. They will give me a sedative as well as the local anaesthetic and if I feel pain at any point I should say so immediately. That is the reassuring bit. Thank goodness there is a reassuring bit since my heart is beginning to race and I am starting to dread the whole thing. The reason for the overnight stay is becoming clearer by the second.

Chris leaves at this point with a few tears in his eyes and I sit in the wheelchair for more clock watching. At 1.45pm they bring my bed and I lay on that for another half an hour while they get everything ready. One of the team inserts a canula effortlessly into my hand. Then at 2.15pm they finally escort me into Room 15 – Radiology. By now my teeth are chattering, more with the chill as with nerves, exacerbated when they swab me with icy cold iodine. I catch a peek at the TV screen which displays nothing more interesting than different views of my liver before they cover me up to my eyes with a sterile blanket.

The sedative calms me down and I don't feel the catheter go in, though there are some unpleasant moments as they guide it through my innards. I speak out each time it hurts and they give me plenty of painkillers via the drip. I have to hold my breath several times during the procedure and it seems to last ages. I don't sleep at all, though I feel quite drowsy throughout which makes it all less frightening.

By late afternoon it is finally over and they transfer me back onto my bed. The nurse from E8 comes down to Radiology and escorts me to the ward. She is given strict instructions that I am to have six hours complete bed rest, which will be until 11pm. They also have to take observations every fifteen until then. Do they imagine I will be up and about at that time of night? Weird.

Chris comes later in the evening though I am quite groggy and can't talk much. They give me a bowl of soup and a roll, which should taste like manna following twelve hours of starvation, but they are horrible. After Chris leaves I have a terrible night. I hardly sleep as the lights are so bright and the noise levels would summon the environmental inspectors in any other context.

At 2am I give up on the idea of sleep. The cacophony of snoring from the adjacent beds provokes murderous thoughts which I resist despite the freedom now to get up. I ask for a painkiller but have to wait forty-five minutes in extreme discomfort before the Sister brings me one, apologising as she was distracted and forgot.

Thank heavens for my Nintendo. I become quite an expert at on screen darts and win ten times.

It is a relief when dawn comes. There are no hot drinks and no sign of breakfast until 9am by which time my stomach is rumbling. It could have saved itself the trouble. The fare is not exactly exciting, or even palatable. One soggy Weetabix biscuit sloshing around aimlessly in a bowl of milk, and a slice of stale bread with marmalade. How are sick people supposed to survive with that standard of nutrition? When I have my operation I will have to get Chris to bring me something I can eat!

The doctors come round half an hour later. A Registrar, whom I had never seen before, tells me they will scan me in four weeks to see if the embolisation has worked. He says I can go home. Before they even leave the ward, I ring Chris and ask him to come up by taxi. I think he hears the desperation verging on tears in my voice, and he is there within the hour.

Fortified by two paracetamol I climb into a taxi just after 10am and we are back in St Helens by 1.30pm.

I am so relieved to be in my own bed this morning. I haven't left it yet!

Epilogue

Dear Lin

I realise this letter is twenty-one years too late, but if I had known in 1987 when your life was so frenetic, what I know now, I think I might have acted differently.

You are so busy, aren't you? I feel for you; I sense your weariness. You get up at the crack of dawn, sort the children for school, organise breakfast, lunchboxes and take them to the childminder. You are at Loughton High by 8am each morning; usually the first arrival and filling the urn before others turn up in the staff room. You teach all day with verve and energy that is uplifting, but sometimes draining. You enjoy your work immensely but the day doesn't end at 4 or 5pm for you. After the staff meeting you rush to pick the children up, take them home, prepare a meal, listen to a blow-by-blow account of Rachel's day, probe to find out what you can about Daniel's day. When the children are settled in bed and the dishwasher loaded, you sit down to work, meticulously preparing lessons, or marking exercise books. Some nights you may enjoy an hour's TV before crawling into bed. You work yourself into a state of utter exhaustion and as the holidays creep closer the tiredness becomes overwhelming. When do you have time for yourself? Time to pursue an enjoyable hobby, or time to read a book? You are on a roller coaster and you just don't know how to stop it. Every job you have had since 1974 has been exactly the same. The job has come first in your life, and everything else has been precariously balanced to fit in around it. Life was slightly less frantic at Carisbrooke, since there were no children to manage, but a longer journey, and equally long hours.

It has taken cancer to force me off the roller coaster. Nothing else would have worked. No one chooses such a devastating disease for themselves, but I am trying to discover what lesson I have to learn from this illness. I think one thing is certain. I needed to stop, and nothing short of cancer would have succeeded. Prior to this I was toying with the idea of an early retirement. Now it is being forced upon me. Whatever the outcome of this operation and treatment I know for certain that I will not return to the workplace. I have done my stint (thirty four years) and deserve a break. I have spent so many years of my life with other folk's children; now I want some time with my own children and grandchildren. I want them to have some benefits from the wisdoms I have gathered over the years.

Whatever time I have left, I will spend it with family and friends, or peaceably pursuing my own interests. I will write, paint, read, play guitar, cycle swim and enjoy myself to the degree that my health permits. No one knows the outcome of this. If I survive the operation, I still have no idea how many years of life it will give me.

So in a sense I will be living each day as it comes, and treating it as a special gift. Cancer is a nasty insidiously quiet disease. It creeps up on you slyly and then smacks you in the gut. But for me, in addition to the fear and the physical discomfort, I have received a wake up call.

I am listening.

Lin Sheffrin
Isle of Wight
2008

Lin's story continues in her blog

http://coloncancerdiary.blogspot.com/

Printed in the United Kingdom by
Lightning Source UK Ltd., Milton Keynes
136761UK00001B/133/P

9 781906 236052